Letting Go

Wil Gritten was raised happily in north Wales without toy guns or television. At sixteen he left home and moved to Brixton under the pretence of becoming a carpenter. Within a year he found himself alone in India, and started writing. Wil stumbled into a career in modelling, and spent a few years working for some of the largest international fashion brands. By the age of twenty-five Wil had circumnavigated the globe twice. He has written for various magazine publications, including *Dazed and Confused*. He writes and records his own unpleasant variety of music and is an expert in the field of organic vegetable gardening. He is currently living in Australia.

Letting Go

Wil Gritten

Parthian
The Old Surgery
Napier Street
Cardigan
SA43 1ED

First published in 2010
© Wil Gritten 2010
All Rights Reserved
ISBN 978-1-905762-76-7

Editor: Lucy Llewellyn
Cover design by Tim Albin www.droplet.co.uk
Inner design & type by Lucy Llewellyn
Printed by Gwasg Gomer, Llandysul

Published with the financial support of the Welsh Books Council.

For your FREE eBook follow these simple steps:
1) find the password: 3rd word on page 11
2) log on to www.parthianbooks.com
3) add 'Letting Go eBook' to your shopping cart
4) add the password when prompted
5) select 'Free order only' option at the checkout
You will then receive an email with a link to your free eBook

British Library Cataloguing in Publication Data
A cataloguing record for this book is available from the British Library.

Lyrics by John Prine used with kind permission from Atlantic Records, by Neil Diamond from Bang Records, by Will Oldham from Drag City, by Mike Ladd from Ozone Music, by Taj Mahal, from Columbia, and by Nick Drake from Island.

For my father

In ancient China there was a young monk who went searching for Buddha. After many years and many hardships the monk found Buddha and asked him the meaning of life. Buddha said nothing, but instead hit the monk on the head – hard, with a stick.
And that was that.

Prologue: Y Ring

In smoky pub-smell mayhem
we weave chaotic pirouettes,
all of us a pretty shining lattice,
all of us a strange and ancient tribe.
The old stagger piston-slow and graceful quiet rhythms
from wooden fireside stool to bar and back,
to and fro in better time than worn-out tickers keep.
Around and between them young men are a frenzied mesh.
A blurred war dance of beer-piss-snort-leer
squareshoulderedstare
spliff-piss-leer-sniff,
on and buzzing on like amphetamine fireflies
in the spasmodic light of the fruit machines.
Beyond them the band are a shapeless, mesmerising altar
to merry grins and stomping legs.
Girls dance a rosy-cheeked alcopop group giggle dance.
They clump like frogspawn here and there
or drape themselves on lucky lads.
Always watching, always giggling.

At beer-spilling midnight we all of us jump and yell
and wish each other enough luck to tide us over.
To tide us over.

Part One

1: A Single Step

They say a journey of a thousand miles starts with a single step. That first step, in the mind of those not doing the stepping, is a bold and noble step, a grand and ceremonial leap into the unknown. That first step is the best step of all, a step to conjure with, the hot step. I don't think they had the train journey between Bangor and Crewe in mind when they coined that phrase.

I'm sitting at a crappy table on a crappy train moving through arguably the crappiest part of the British Isles. Thousands of caravans stand to attention outside my window like plastic–aluminium recruits in a drizzly grey parade bound for nowhere. I am Major W. Hooper surveying my crappy troops. I am commander general of a stunted army of part-time homes for crappy factory fortnight Scousers and Brummies. I am scorn. I am judgement. I am bound far away.

Sharing this sorry scene with me are some young Christian band camp delegates who cheerfully piled onto the train at Colwyn Bay. They politely asked me if the seats around me were taken. Though evidently they were not, I tried, with facial expressions alone, to convey to them that perhaps they were. My ego's sitting here, and next to it sits my fear of arriving in Caracas as green and innocent as any gringo ever was. On the next table sit my repressed homesickness, my self-consciousness and my hatred of happy Christian soldiers. They're all sitting quite comfortably, can't you see them?

Evidently they could not, so down they sat.

They are excruciatingly polite. They keep smiling at me and baby-talking to each other about who's going to be playing whose instrument this year and what Tarquin said about Sarah's saxophone. I stuff heavy metal headphones into my ears and practise every savage expression I can muster. Frustratingly none of this has any effect on them, the forgiving bastards.

Mercifully they leave the train in Chester, bound for band camp and eventually heaven, eternal light and the singing of a hundred million angels. I am bound for Euston.

A memory of New Year's Eve, a few days before, comes back to me. I was slumped in a drunken booth when an old friend, Rhys Anwyl, appeared before me; a loveable apparition in farmer's tan and primary school memory.

'Why are you going away, Wil?' he'd asked, dark humorous eyes.

'Because I feel like I have things to learn about myself and the world. To grow.' I'd said, being smart.

'Why are you going away, Wil?' he'd asked again. His whole life: sheep and mountains and family.

'Because I need to get a past before I can settle down to a future,' I'd said. My whole life: a wandering happenstance.

'Why are you going away, Wil?' he asked, again.

'Because I need to find a good woman,' I'd said. The truth, one of them.

Just then straw haired healthy farmer's wife took dark

haired healthy farmer by the arm and dragged him doorwards. He smiled. I smiled.

'I'll see you when you get back then,' he said.

'Okay,' I said.

And that was that.

The drained winter countryside turns into the orange glow of Euston, Euston turns into the Victoria line, the Victoria line turns into Brixton, Brixton into Coldharbour Lane.

The Prince Albert, where I spent two manic years as a lowly assistant manager, is warm and pleased to see me. I soon quit moaning to my friend Lucy about needing food and settle into drinking and meeting old friends instead, some of whom I've forgotten even existed in the two months I've spent holed up in my folks' house in Wales.

Every now and then I catch myself habitually scanning the place for thieves, crack heads and trouble, even though it's not my job any more. My Welsh rehab session hasn't extracted all of Brixton out of me, but I'm different, stronger and purer of heart than when I worked here. The pub seems less dingy, the crack heads less aggressive, the danger less obvious, my defences less necessary. Soon it all melds together into a swimming mosaic of drunken warmth and colour and sin. I don't belong here any more. I am bound far away. This place is a pleasantly static stepping stone and I am bound far away.

2: Providence

Providence, Rhode Island, is swaddled and brittle under a metre of fresh snow. The wind is a biting minus 15°C, every breath is a steaming geyser and the sidewalks are treacherous runways of black ice. Even the statues seem to shiver it's so bloody cold.

Cleverly I am wearing flimsy Dunlop Green Flash, perfect for falling over and hurting myself as much as possible. I'm numb now though, bone cold to the core, so I don't care so much. Welcome to stage three of hypothermia.

I'm on my way back to Manhattan. The roads are finally open, though this shabby, teeth-chattering crowd waiting for the bus with me don't seem too convinced.

I left Manhattan behind three days ago in search of quieter climes. My ex-girlfriend Frances' apartment was just too small and noisy. Two guinea pigs, a ginger flatmate, herself, myself and all our baggage, emotional and otherwise, crammed into two small rooms with heating pipes steaming and whistling incessantly. Someone attempted at some point to fix a broken steam valve by tying a sock around it. Steam still came hissing and spluttering out. Smelling of sock. I had to get out.

I caught the Greyhound north and tried desperately to defrost my feet as gloomy housing projects gave way to old wooden houses, icicles hanging from their roofs. It was dark by the time the bus arrived in Providence. I jiggled and skipped about trying to keep warm while I waited for my lift. Down by the bus stop an old woman was struggling ineffectually with a pile of suitcases. I wandered over to give her a hand. She looked a bit scared of me at first (I was wearing a balaclava), but it was so cold I think she would have let a bear help her.

She was wearing sandals and socks, a good twenty layers of summer dresses and several woolly hats. I asked her where she'd come from. Her English wasn't too good but it soon became clear that she'd come all the way from central Africa that day – all the way from 35°C to minus 15°C. A temperature change of 50°c. She looked shell-shocked and completely disorientated – said her family were picking her up. I ushered her into the bus station to keep warm and sat outside with her bags and smoked a ciggie.

When Paul and Sarah pulled up in their pick-up I left my Samaritan post, asking an entirely uninterested guard to keep an eye on the old woman, and jumped in the back. I love these guys. They're old friends of my folks, ageing hippies and musicians by trade and temperament; their feet tap in time with every conversation, pleased as punch that I've made the effort to come and say hi.

Paul was harmonica world champ back in '76 – an English public schoolboy made good. His lively eyes sparkle behind little round specs and his whole face is ringed by a healthy Jew-fro. I imagine Sarah hasn't changed since she was about nine – crazy blond curls, a fiddle and a will of iron.

It started snowing as soon as I got there and didn't let up for days. We spent our time eating, drinking, shovelling and playing. Look – there's me strumming away on the guitar hoping neither of them can hear the mess I'm making. There's Sarah stomping about the place thrashing at the fiddle and Paul yelling out chords to me, while effortlessly alternating between the harmonica in his mouth and the banjo on his knee.

That guy next door to Frances' place in Manhattan, who starts his loud TV-watching and wife-berating sessions nice and early, would be gently run out of town by the good folks of Providence. Yee ha.

At the bus station my Greyhound back to Manhattan pulls up a full hour late. By this time we, the shabby waiters, have united. We have formed bonds. We are now not just a pack of cold individuals, we are a cold and angry mob. We have communicated!

'Someone should do something,' said someone.

'Yeah,' someone else agreed. We all agreed.

Now we huddle together as the door hisses open. We have unanimously elected a spokesperson in a vote without words.

That funny looking guy at the front of the line will speak for us. He will be our voice. The door hisses open. We crowd behind our great leader. The mist clears. Standing in the doorway is the biggest, strangest, campest looking guy I've ever seen. He is a huge gay Goliath. About his mighty girth is tied a belt of purest leatherette cutting him in two betwixt his huge and sagging arse and his pendulous belly. We gasp and step back. The colossus swings his mighty hands onto his bulging hips and purses his momentous lips. He knows that we are not happy. He knows that there will be complaints. He is ready.

'Ahem,' our gracious and courageous leader clears his throat. Here come the words of the people, the righteous stone in David's sling, the great leveller –

'Um, will you be going via Boston, sir?'

'Hell no!' booms the unholy voice. 'You at the wrong stop honey! Now, if you all wanna be in New York City by tonight you better stop playin' around and get on the bus. Who's first?'

And with that we are beaten. We shuffle onto the bus, our heads bowed. Dejectedly we hand over our trembling tickets. Our once glorious leader slopes off to find the right bus stop and we eye his passing with mutinous contempt.

I settle into my seat and practise my Spanish numbers, quietly shivering. I cast my mind back to Wales and the Christian band camp delegates. They're like a little log fire burning in my mind and I drift off to sleep warmed by them.

The next day Frances and I decide to eat the mushrooms I'd sent over from Wales in the autumn. It's still snowing outside. We sit on the subway wrapped in layer upon layer of jackets and scarves and hats looking like Joseph and his Technicolour Michelin men. My guts turn familiar somersaults as enzymes break down drugs and feed them through my eager blood stream into my jet-lagged brain. By the time we squelch up the sodden, dirty steps into the steaming street I can see the first funny twitches in my vision and feel the first grins tugging at my cheeks.

The Metropolitan Museum of Art is crowded. Seventeen-foot security guards rumble around like elephants in black suits. Japanese tourists gamble in the undergrowth like packs of chattering monkeys. We drift apart in this sea of faces and echoing halls, occasionally to meet in front of Georgia O'Keefe and giggle at her tulip's clitoris. I find myself standing in front of a vase of sunflowers: its lines and shapes are made of twisting worms, and suddenly I understand. I am different now. I am serene. The other people here have no idea what they are looking at. Their shallow, three-dimensional minds can only grasp pathetically at the depth of these paintings but I, I am inside.

I leave this borrowed meat for a while and merge with oil and turpentine. I walk old Paris trailing short-sighted lily pads. I sit under a twisting grove of trees and whisper sweet nothings into the brown ears of pert-breasted Tahitian girls, while angels hide in the bushes and blush and giggle. I cry over hair and skin tone and sea-smashed rigging while all around me camera phones click and dumb tourists say dumb tourist things. I am oblivious. I am six-dimensional: three of space, two of time and an extra one, an emotional one, which keeps me skipping through the undergrowth as happy and as earnest as a lamb.

Then it's over. Closing time at the zoo. The MET politely ejects us using its security elephants like fat fingers on the ends of shiny corridor arms and once again we're back in snowy Central Park wandering and wondering, lost again in tone and colour.

That night I made a fool of myself. I don't remember it all. There was a bag of coke which I bought and then refused to take or share. There were Zanex.

I called Frances' new boyfriend an alcoholic. I told Frances' flatmate that she might be happier if she got off the anti-depressants and stopped being her mother. God only knows what I told Frances.

I had seen things, you see. I thought I could help but I don't think people like having their faults aired openly, especially not by bearded, drunk, tripping, half-feral Welshmen they hardly know. I can't imagine why not.

Perhaps it would be better to say that I was jealous of Frances' new boyfriend and unable to deal with the situation. Perhaps it would be better still to let it all go – to simply say I woke up feeling sheepish and that my sense of sheepishness grew and grew until I politely made my excuses and, prompted in no uncertain terms by Frances, left for Caracas and warmth and the unknown. A week early.

3: Puerto Rico

I smell. Two flights and a 04:00 start, not to mention the drug and alcohol abuse of the last few weeks, have left me a bit pongy. As countrified as I get in the country, I still have a social conscience when it comes to being in close proximity to my fellow, deodorised man. I showered before leaving Frances' sleeping apartment and my shirt was clean on this morning. I'm not so inconsiderate that I'd get on a plane smelly.

That doesn't matter much now though. I stink. The captain says Caracas is a balmy 32°C. Things can only get worse. The young Latino couple sitting next to me politely moved to a safer aisle a few minutes after the seat belt signs were turned off. 'Please make sure your own mask is fitted before helping others.'

My hatred and rage at Bush's US of A is leaking out of me like so much defrosted freezer gunk. I almost cried with relief at leaving the Fourth Reich, so upset was I by its extremes and propaganda. Descending into Puerto Rico International felt like reaching dry land after swimming through a lake of poisonous jellyfish. The bird has flown from the cage. The eagle is landing. Freedom here we come!

Sadly I was wrong. Very wrong. Taco Bell and Starbucks feature queues as wide as they are long. Think Brits abroad, only heavier and louder, dumbed down, waving small American flags. It looks like some crazy bastard has dressed up a bunch of manatees in bad clothes and let them lumber around in public. Little Puerto Rican waiters flit about like suckerfish as these leviathan forms bellow for super-sized fries and buckets of sweet milkshake thickened with the fat of chickens.

Oh, Captain Ahab! This is your wet dream. Get that painted savage Quequeg up there on the escalator with a sharpened iron and a potted line and let's drag a few barrels home to old Nantucket! Heave ho, my boys!

4: Caracas

Well here we are: Caracas. Jungle hills falling haphazardly into the sea, dusted like green Christmas cakes with rubbish from the barrios which perch like potter wasp nests, bristling satellite dishes and antennae.

I still smell, but that doesn't seem to matter now because it's seat belt time and we swing round and come in low and fast over the waves, and bump and screech and break and reverse engines, and slow and slow and turn her round towards the little airport building.

'Please wait until the aircraft has come to a complete standstill before unfastening your seatbelts.'

I shouldn't be this scared. I should be coping better. I

winged it though two dead bodies and a bout of septicaemia in India and Sri Lanka when I was eighteen. I survived two insane months with my old mate Gwyds in Madagascar when I was twenty-one. I've worked in all sorts of crazy places around the world, from Cape Town to Tokyo to darkest North Wales. I've lived and worked on Coldharbour Lane among the crack dealers and smackheads for years. I should not be this scared. But I am.

My arrival here has been built up so much in my mind by my well-meaning friends and relatives with their well-meaning advice:

'Watch out for the rapists and the kidnappers, Wil,' they'd say helpfully, 'and the thieves and the murderers and the coppers.'

'Ooo yeah Wil, the coppers, they're the worst.'

'Yeah Wil, I heard the coppers kidnap you, rob you then sell you to the rapists who rape you and then murder you.'

'Ooo yeah, I heard that too, Wil. Where is it you're going again?'

My own imagination, though I try to relax and be positive, makes up reams of horror stories too, mostly centring on being mugged. I have learned next to nothing about this country or its language. I have learnt to count in Spanish. That is all. What am I doing?

I can't forget my Brazilian friend Paula's face when I told her I was starting my trip in Caracas.

'*Caraio*, Weeel,' in that crazy São Paulo accent, 'you must be fucking crazy maan. Caracas is dangerous for you.'

'C'mon Paula,' I'd said, 'I'm not that soft. I can handle myself.'

I can, can't I? I have survived so far through some pretty tough situations. But was that my doing? Was that me handling it or was I just lucky? Like that time my mate Gwyds and that South African girl got held hostage for desecrating the memory of Queen Ranavalona. It was pure luck that we managed to sort that out. How many other near misses have been pure luck?

God! If people had just left me alone before I arrived here maybe I wouldn't be shitting myself quite as much as I am. But what if people hadn't warned me about the dangers of this place? Maybe I'd be skipping happily into the lions' den without a care in the world. And we must take care, in a world as nasty as this, mustn't we Willy?

The first thing that strikes me is how small the airport is, it's like a local domestic airport. I'd imagined something grander. A Mexico City scene: massive, sprawling and overpoweringly South American. In reality it's rather quaint. Just a couple of runways squatting by the sea and a square, white terminal dwarfed by lush, green hills. My heart is pounding just looking at them. The fact that I'm willingly walking into this trap seems ludicrous. As we disembark I give myself a talking to:

Now Wil, I say, in my head, keep your eyes open, stay sharp and don't miss a trick. But relax and go with it. You are comfortable man, comfortable.

I am not comfortable. To give myself time to get comfortable I charitably decided, while still in New York, to go straight to Los Roques, a little group of islands out in the Caribbean sea north of Venezuela.

To get there I need to change money. I need to find the domestic terminal. I need to buy myself a ticket to the islands. If I can't get a flight today I need to go to central Caracas, find a cheap hotel, sleep there and come back the next day. Above all I need to not get ripped off, mugged, murdered, raped, kidnapped or coppered. For this I need to be on my toes and to not be such a day-glo gringo. Right. Here goes. I sit down on my pack outside the terminal and roll a ciggie. It is hot, not overwhelmingly so, but a damn sight hotter than New York. Hot enough to send a constant, sluggish river of sweat down my back.

I light my ciggie, inhaling deeply and rolling slightly from the head rush. I close my eyes and sit there sweating and swaying. When I open them a wolfish Latino with a gold tooth is standing over me.

'You need any help, man? You wanna change some money?'

Aha. I think. Here we go. This guy thinks I'm a sucker.

'No.'

'You American, man?'

'No.' Huh – imagine – me – a Yank!

I squint and spit, doing it like no sucker ever did.

'If you wanna change money do it on the black market, man, do it with me,' he says. 'Don't go to those crooks, man, they'll rip you off.'

He points towards Thomas Cook with a heavily ringed finger, I look over. There's old Tommy, shining with cleanliness and western promise, complete with meek, uniformed Latina and flashy currency board.

I see what you're doing, I think at him, but it ain't gonna work, man.

'Hmmm,' I say and take an uninterested puff on my ciggie.

'Okay man,' he says, 'like I said, If you need anything you come and find me. I can sort you some good tickets to the islands too.'

I squint into the distance like I don't have time to think about that sort of thing. He shrugs.

'Okay, *ciao*, man,' he says, and walks away.

Ha! I think, squint, spit, I showed him.

I shoulder my pack and start looking for the domestic terminal. I wander around asking people if they speak English.

They don't. One guy in an internet café does a bit but when I follow his directions I end up in the bus station. By now I'm sweating like a pig and the squinting and spitting routine is getting a bit much.

I go back to the main terminal and sit back in my original spot and roll another ciggie. I am a much more dishevelled and sweaty gringo that when I was first here. Pathetic is waiting just around the corner, close. I close my eyes and take some deep breaths. You can do this, Willy. You've done this so many times before. Just imagine, in a couple of weeks you're going to be an old pro again. Just relax, let go and keep…

'You need any help, man?'

I open my eyes and look up at him. He's standing above me again, gold tooth glinting in the sun.

'Yes,' I say, 'yes I do.'

He wasn't so bad, old Wolf Boy, I'd imagined he'd be much worse. He helped me out. He got me a mediocre price for my traveller's cheques, a better price than old Tommy Cook by far but still a mediocre price. He also got me a decent ticket to Los Roques for the following day, showed where to catch the bus to central Caracas and he gave me some useful advice:

'Don't look at the cops, don't talk to the cops and don't roll your own cigarettes in front of the cops. We don't do that here. They will fucking bust you, weed or not.'

The whole time I didn't believe a word he said. The whole time I was convinced he was ripping me off. The whole time I tried to cover my nervousness and yellow-bellied greenness with feigned disinterest and arrogance. Poor Wolf Boy. I didn't mean to be rude. I was just scared.

Outside the tinted windows of the airport bus is Venezuela. Old busted Cadillacs and Buicks cruise by full of swarthy looking *hombres malos*. There are army trucks everywhere, roadblocks complete with soldiers in jungle cammo and M16s.

The barrios are incredible close-up. Entire hillsides covered in buildings piled impossibly on top of each other, washing lines and electric wires strung between them billowing brightly coloured dresses and baseball shirts. Huge satellite dishes poke from the roofs of tiny shacks like strange fungi. Kids fly kites made of plastic bags and everywhere there is laughter and shouting, everywhere music and rubbish.

I am amazed. I am slack-jawed gringo awe-struck dumb. I am gawping out the window like a five-year-old. Then I remember myself and shut my gob, look around to see if anyone's noticed and go back to my dead-eyed squint. But still I am amazed.

My bus stop is called Gato Negro – which means Black Cat. I have drawn myself a map on a scrap of paper for fear of looking like a tourist with my guide book. The map shows the tube station I have to get off at and the hotel I've decided to stay in. I also have a small compass so I can discreetly take a bearing and therefore won't get lost. I feel like a fucking commando now. Preparation. Preparation. Preparation.

The bus stops for the first time. The street is busy with market traffic and schoolchildren. It can't be my stop. I don't see a subway anywhere. I catch the eye of a dark, shady looking guy in the seat behind me and ask lamely:

'*Por favor, es Gato Negro?*'

'I dunno what you're saying, mate,' he says in a strong Aussie accent, 'I don't speak Spanish.'

'Jesus,' I say, shocked to hear English spoken in this world of savages, 'I don't either.'

'*Si Señor. Gato Negro es aquí,*' the girl sitting next to me says, pointing downward.

I scramble off the bus, grabbing my rucksack and yelling emotionally at the Aussie guy I never even met: 'It was nice to meet you!'

And then I'm alone again. But there's the tube and there's me on it, checking my compass and map, casting furtive glances at the decidedly ordinary-looking passengers. There's my stop and there's that gringo (me) with a backpack, a compass and a crappy map on a crappy scrap of paper in that crappy downtown street, somewhere in South America.

Sabana Grande. It's all crack and market stalls, pirate DVDs and dodgy bastards. But it's not so bad. In fact it's a bit like Brixton. Except everybody speaks Spanish and the coppers don't have the decency to pretend legitimacy. At least that's what I'm told.

I stand by the philosophy that if I make myself look like less of a victim than any other victim I'll be alright. As long as there's an easier target than me then I'll be OK. However, when there are no easier targets about, like now, philosophy number two has to be utilised: mad people are not easy targets. So with that in mind I lurch off down the road with a slight tick, a gammy leg, a compass, a crappy map and a rucksack, in the wrong direction.

Eventually, just as night is falling, I find the Nuestro Hotel. Without, I might add, being mugged, kidnapped, harassed, harangued, murdered, raped or put upon in any way. Whether that is because I'm lucky or because I look convincingly insane I will never know. I imagine it's a bit of a mixture.

My chosen refuge is a two storey terraced house of crumbling plaster and red tile. The bottom floor is entirely encased in an iron cage. Hung on the bars of this cage is a board which advertises weekly, nightly or hourly rates.

The buzzer at the front gate attracts a shuffling little old man who, after ascertaining that I understand absolutely nothing he is saying, lets me in. There is a little garden full of noisy parrots, a fat old woman eyeing me suspiciously and two rucksacks stacked against the wall. Never have I been so glad to see evidence of fellow travellers. I am not alone!

So here I am again. Lying on my back looking up at the ceiling fan in a dirty little hotel room in the sticky centre of all that is vastly unfamiliar, foreign and unknown.

Somehow, though, I feel at home. Somehow I feel like I never really left this room. Somehow it's the same room I was in when I got sick in India, crying and shitting and puking for a week.

It's the same room I've been in a million times before. It is me, me stripped down to just me and nothing more. Me and a bag full of naïve, innocent possessions; relics of a childlike time just twenty-four hours ago.

If it wasn't for tonight's company of veterans and easier targets I think I would be having a much harder time being so romantic about my situation. As it is I am drunk.

Ice cold cans of Polar beer with pictures of sexy chicks in bikinis on the side. Duty free fags and plastic chairs. Lonely Planets and Rough Guides and bum bags and Walkman speakers and

'Hello, I am Helga from Sweden and this is Lottie.'

'Hi, I'm Wil.'

And this is BB, a tall, Jesus-looking German; Carlos, a befreckled Costa Rican/Swiss kid; and Delores, a pale skinned, dyed-black haired, half Mexican Yank with blue poetry tattooed on her white inner arms and a pair of boots as large and out of proportion with the rest of her as her sense of melancholic angst. I like her immediately.

And so I lay me down to sleep. I pray that tomorrow I won't be raped, murdered, robbed or set upon in any other vile way. If I should be any of the above before I wake, I pray I stand a fighting chance or die quickly.

Amen.

5: Puerto La Cruz

At a sand-carved wooden bench on a sun-bleached beach I sit, staring down at my white feet, the hair on my toes. A fly half-heartedly explores the red imprint left by my sweaty sock. Into the calm shallows a pelican plops, and when it surfaces again its throat pouch resembles a taut cow's udder, sloshing full of little fish.

The sea sucks in, the sea spits out.

I am out of place, white as alabaster, sickly for a moment when the village girl passed my rucksack, my sweaty socks, my white feet, my inability to move or make sense of this scene, this paradise, this trap.

Behind me is a village. In the future I will sit in the plaza there. For an hour I will just sit, as an experiment in trust, to prove once and for all that if I just sit and wait and relax then the universe will provide. And all I need is to be patient. And relax and wait. Let go.

In the present I listen to the pelicans plop and the sea suck. Behind me is the world I had least expected: a world of tourists. Italian tourists with too much money, with cellulite and Gucci flip flops. Italian tourists by the hundred. In the past I had no idea they'd be here. In the past I was shocked and disappointed and sat on a bench to watch my toes. In the present I'm still watching my toes. I'm still shocked, still disappointed, still sitting on this bench.

In the future I will get up wearily and put my sweaty socks in my shoes, then I will tie the shoes to my pack, roll up my trouser legs and ask surly, tourist-tired locals the prices of rooms I can't afford. After that I will sit in the plaza and watch the people. I will relax and tell myself that all I need to do is let go, and I will believe myself. I will relax my shoulders and I will smile.

The Italians will not understand, but that won't matter at all, because I will sit for an hour and smile. Then I will meet Chris and Chloe and the universe will tell me I did good because they know a guy I know, who kissed Frances after we broke up. In the past.

In the present I don't know any of this. In the present I'm shocked and disappointed.

I look down at my white feet, and the fly on my toe, and the red sock imprints, and listen to the pelicans plop and the sea suck.

High above the Caribbean Sea, flying back from Los Roques in a jumpy little biplane, I'm talking to myself again.

You did good there, Willy, I say, and I beam and glow inside. *You did good. You can do this. You spent more money than you would have liked but that's okay. You've survived so far and you've survived well. You're on the right track. Keep chilling and keep your eyes open. I'm so proud of you.*

I snuggle back into my cramped bucket seat and watch the white-caps far below, trying to gauge the size of the swell. The plane jumps and bucks and the Italian Gucci tourists around me murmur nervously but I feel only a pleasant lurch of adrenaline. I'm loose, I'm lucid, I'm surviving. A few heavy raindrops smack against the windshield and suddenly the sky ahead and the sea below vanish in a roar of grey water. The co-pilot turns in his seat and yells something in Spanish over the noise, presumably something reassuring. The Italians groan and chatter among themselves. I smile inwardly and watch the flimsy windscreen wipers and the side of the pilot's face – as long as he looks as bored as he does I've got nothing to worry about.

Lightning cracks up ahead, rain hammers the windows and the little plane rears and dives, rears and dives and all I feel is pleasant excitement and a warm certainty that all shall be well. The pilot remains as bored as ever, the Gucci tourists turn to jelly, water leaks through a hole above the co-pilot's head and drips rhythmically onto his faded cap, soundless in the roar of the wind and the howl of the engines. Then, as suddenly as we were sucked into the storm, we're spat out again and ahead the green jungle hills of the Venezuelan coast roll off into the distance, among them the anthills of Caracas, from here no less a part of nature, just another colour. The pilot's expression doesn't change once.

Back at the Nuestro Hotel in Sabana Grande, caged once again with the squabbling parrots and suspicious old women, I attempt courageously to order a room in Spanish. After ten minutes of misunderstood questions and malformed statements the cage opens and BB, the German guy I met before, walks in. He looks older than he did three days ago, tired and drawn but no less Jesus-like, perhaps more so.

'Hey Jesus!' I say.

'Hey Wil,' he nods, flopping down on a bench, leaning his head against the peeling baby blue of the wall.

'¿Cerveza?' asks the old man behind the counter.

'Gracias,' says BB, taking the can and holding it against his forehead for a second before opening it.

'What's the matter?' I ask him, taking another beer from the old man, sliding money for both over the counter. My beer has a picture of a girl in a bikini on the side; a caption underneath says her name is 'Cynthia'. I open Cynthia and take a swig; she's cool and lovely. Apart from Cynthia the only cool part of me is the line of sweat down my back. It's a scorcher out there.

'Fucking passport,' BB is saying. 'You know I was robbed two weeks ago?' I shake my head. 'Well they took all my shit. I spent all morning with the cops getting a crime number and all afternoon at the embassy sorting out a passport. They're all fucking bastards.'

'Sucks to be you,' I tell him helpfully and we sit like that for a while, sipping and sighing, listening to the parrots and the traffic and the hum of the fan. The old man goes back to reading his paper.

'Will you ask him if there's a room for me?' I ask BB.

'We've got a spare bed in our room,' he says, 'you can have that.' He says something to the old man that I don't understand. The old man grunts an affirmative and, without looking up from his paper, hooks a key from a rack and hands it to me.

I follow BB upstairs to the room. He points at a bunk. 'That's you,' he says, 'that's me and that's Carlos,' pointing at the other two in turn.

I hump my pack on the bed and creak down next to it. It's hotter in here than outside.

'What are you doing for carnival?' BB asks from the bathroom, then he turns the shower on and I have to shout over the noise.

'I dunno,' I shout. 'When's carnival?'

'This weekend,' he shouts back. I don't know what day it is.

'What day is it?' I shout. There's a pause. I imagine him counting his fingers.

'Thursday.'

'Oh,' I shout. He comes out of the shower covered in goose pimples looking pleased with himself.

'I take a cold shower at least five times a day,' he says. 'If I didn't I would die.'

'Good idea.' I drag myself up.

'I have to go back to the embassy now,' he says, spraying himself with something noxious. 'I'll be back in a couple of hours. Lock the room up when you go.'

'Cheers BB,' I call from the shower. I don't hear what he says back because my head's under the water, gasping for breath, cold water shocking my cerebellum back to life.

Cool and relaxed but warming up fast I wander downstairs for more beer and then back upstairs to sit on the balcony and read. Delores is sitting there already, her pale little face buried in Kerouac, her feet up on a plastic chair.

'Beer?' I ask after sitting down, holding out my spare can.

'Thanks,' she says, taking it from me. 'What were the islands like?'

'Paradise,' I reply. 'Crawling with tourists, dripping with money.'

'That's a shame,' she says.

The girl on my can is called Maria now. She's wearing a yellow one-piece with sexy holes cut out of it. I open Maria. She's even nicer than Cynthia was. Delores pushes a pack of Marlboro red towards me with her toe.

'Cheers,' I say. She looks at me funny. 'It means "thank you" in English', I explain. She just raises her eyebrows and goes back to her book. I open mine and read the same paragraph three times, not taking it in. I put it back down on my lap and light one of her Marlboros. The air is so thick with heat and pollution it's like sucking on an exhaust pipe. I exhale and close my eyes, holding Maria to my forehead with my other hand.

'Can I ask you something, Wil?' I open my eyes, Delores is watching me. The deadpan expression is gone from her face, she looks much younger without it.

'Uh huh,' I grunt.

'Do you get scared?' She looks me directly in the eye.

'Of what?' I ask, wondering whether or not to lie.

'Of this,' she says, waving a finger at the mayhem of Caracas, 'you know? Travelling, being alone, being so far away from home and anything normal...'

She lets her sentence trail off, the list could have gone on for hours. I sigh and sit forward, glancing down at the cigarette in my hand.

'Yes,' I say simply. 'Terrified.'

She smiles.

'But it's okay, you know?' I say, smiling too, opening up to her. 'I talk to myself. I tell myself I'm okay. I've been travelling for years and I still get just as scared as I did when I was younger, but now I know it passes. Now I know that if I just relax and try not to be too hard on myself I get by. I get a high from facing my fear, and that makes it all worthwhile... but I do spend a lot of time shitting myself.'

'I'm so glad you said that,' she looks like she might cry, but she's smiling too, 'I thought I might be the only one. Stupid I guess.'

'Not stupid,' I say and I'm surprised by how gentle my voice sounds. 'Stupid is never facing your fear. Stupid is stuck in a small town dying of boredom and daytime TV. Stupid isn't out in Caracas alone trying to achieve something it can't see and doesn't understand.'

Then I stop because that does sound a bit stupid, there's been a voice in my head suggesting as much since I booked my ticket.

She laughs. I look up, see that she's not laughing at me and I laugh too.

'Well,' I say, 'okay, maybe a bit stupid, but good stupid, character-building stupid, brave stupid.'

'Empowered stupid,' she says.

'Yeah,'

We both smile and look around us for a minute, at Caracas whizzing by, at the hills beyond, at the deep, hazy blue of the sky.

'What are you doing for carnival?' I ask after a while.

'Nothing,' she says. 'When's carnival?'

By all accounts carnival in Caracas is a non-event. It's not like São Paulo or Rio, not even like Notting Hill. Instead of parading the streets in bikinis and peacock feathers the populace pack their cars with cool boxes and scanty swimwear and head for the relative cool of the beaches.

The better prepared among the few tourists in the city have booked rooms by the beach, well in advance, and are on their way long before the roads get too jammed. The marginally less well prepared are booked onto buses and are bustling around, packing and making plans. They're a chirpy bunch, the marginals, with their near future half-planned and neatly arranged before them.

Then there are the ones who aren't prepared at all. The ones who are still sitting about drinking cold beer and reading books as the last of the marginals leave. The ones whose future is an utter mystery. The ones destined to be left behind. Us.

Carlos, Delores and I are taking it easy, ignoring the advice of the well-prepareds and marginals, sitting with our feet up, enjoying the polluted sunshine. Delores is reading, Carlos and I are discussing beer.

'Cynthia's nice but I prefer Maria,' I tell Carlos. He nods his freckly head sagely and purses his lips.

'What you say is wise,' he says slowly, 'but...' He leans

forward, triumphantly holding out his can, 'have you met Evelina?'

'Shit,' I say, he's got me; Evelina is truly a fine piece of work. She's busting out of a minimal white crocheted number, skin moist, lips slightly parted in ecstasy. Carlos sits back in his chair and slurps Evelina with obvious satisfaction.

'You guys suck,' says Delores without looking up.

The stairs creak and BB wanders onto the balcony looking worse than he did earlier. He flops down and opens a beer. His beer is called Evelina too. He doesn't even notice.

'Well,' he says, 'I have a passport, but it cost me my sanity.'

'Good,' says Carlos, not quite understanding.

'What now then?' asks Delores, putting her book down. Nobody answers. We're totally unprepared for questions like that.

'We should go to the beach,' says me.

'Which beach?' asks Carlos.

'Dunno,' says me. 'Shall we look at a map?'

The next day, after an epic two hour slog across the city (which was only supposed to be a fifteen minute stroll), we arrive, bedraggled and sweaty, at a bus terminal. After queuing for a further forty minutes we reach the booking window and a scrawny youth in pimply shirt and tie who looks a lot like Mel Gibson, only baggier and entirely uncharismatic. Delores asks him for four tickets to Choroni, an idyllic fishing village over the mountains from Maracay. He looks at her as if she's asked him to take his pecker out and turn it into the Eiffel Tower. Delores turns to us, her pale little brow creased in a frown. The guy behind us in the queue coughs impatiently.

'No go?' I ask. Obviously not. I dig in my pack for a guidebook and a map. Then I start reeling off the names of every beach town along the coast. Each time Mel Gibson shakes his head pityingly.

'Has he actually got any tickets to anywhere at all?' I ask eventually. Delores translates. Mel checks his computer. The guy behind us looks up at the ceiling pleadingly. Mel looks up with a surprised expression on his gawky face then scribbles something down on a piece of paper and slides it under the glass.

'Got something?' BB asks.

'Kinda,' says Delores, reading the piece of paper. 'We have to go to another bus terminal. Has anyone heard of Puerto La Cruz?'

The bus is cold. It seems to be a status symbol in Venezuela: the richer you are, the more powerful your bus's air conditioning is. The really rich must be driving around in freezer trucks with icicles hanging off their noses.

The boys sit together near the front and Dolores and I share her sleeping bag in the middle somewhere. Later on we share my headphones too and when she gets tired Dolores asks me if she can sleep on my shoulder. I listen to Bonnie 'Prince' Billy and watch oil towers burning waste gas in the darkness and her hair smells funny, greasy and not all that nice, but it feels good to touch someone, good to have someone touch me.

I drift off, wake up, drift off again, wonder what fate has in store for us at the other end, wonder why I'm not one of the prepared ones, wonder where it will all lead, wonder why I always have to go blindly into the darkness.

At midnight, with no idea what's going on, we arrive in Puerto La Cruz. The four of us stand around, bleary eyed, waiting for our luggage, yawning and smoking nasty-tasting cigarettes. There are no other tourists on our bus.

An odd looking man in a dirty paisley pullover and stained slacks sidles up to us. I don't like the look of him so I don't look at him. Instead I take a step towards Delores so he won't look at her. Wringing his hands and licking his lips he walks up to Carlos. Carlos says hello to the guy, the guy says hello to Carlos, and then they start talking together in Spanish.

Our packs retrieved, we walk to an empty bench to decide what to do next. I'm fighting lethargy and fuzziness out of my brain so I can make decisions. The greasy-slack guy follows us. I open my pack and pull out my guidebook – might as well do it the easy way. The guy licks his lips. Carlos steps forward.

Please don't... I beg him in my head but he does:

'This guy says he knows a place we can go,' says Carlos. I look around. The bus station is dark and stinking, diesel fumes and stray dogs, tramps and taxi drivers.

'Do you think that's a good idea?' I ask Carlos. My tone says that I don't.

'Well,' Carlos says grumpily, 'what else are we going to do?'

'There's a hotel two blocks from here,' I say, looking at the little map. 'We can walk.' I look at BB and Delores. They nod. Carlos sighs. He turns to Slack-man and says something mildly apologetic. Slack-man doesn't look happy. Carlos turns to me with a pleading look on his face. I'm too tired for this. Too tired and lost and scared to have much patience left. But not so tired I can be led into an alley like Chicken Licken and robbed by a man in a paisley pullover. I suddenly remember a helpful statistic someone told me a couple of days ago: one in four people in Venezuela regularly carries a handgun.

'No,' I say quickly, snapping out of it. 'No, no, fuck no. Listen,' I say to Slack-man-Foxy-Loxy, 'fuck off, we'll be just fine. Tell him BB. C'mon you lot, it'll be fine. Sorry Carlos but I'm not going with that guy. Right. Packs on. Let's go!'

And we're out of the bus station and onto the street before

any of them can say a word. Only then do I realise that we might have a little more to fear than just Foxy Loxy. Down the street ahead of us, in full drunken glory, is Gangy Langy – shadows flickering on the walls, shouts and screams echoing eerily among our footsteps.

'Right!' I say cheerily, 'Not that way.'

It is that way. But we're not going that way.

We avoid the drunken gang scene and skirt a few blocks over, walking fast with our heads up, cracking jokes and laughing just to show everyone that we're not completely, entirely, overwhelmingly terrified. Carlos mutters something about getting us all killed but the others seem to get it. We turn a corner and ahead of us, past only a few drunks and a screaming baby, is a neon sign flashing 'Hotel'.

I wait outside with Delores while the lads go in and check if there's any room. A few metres away two guys are chatting by a little food cart. One of them sees us and nudges the other one, who looks round and then motions us to come over. I look at Delores. If I just ignore him it'll seem as if I'm scared. If I go over I won't understand a word he says.

'Hey,' he calls over in English, 'you come here.' I shrug, wink at Delores and turn around.

'Hello,' I say, calm, non-committal, half-smiling.

'American?' He asks, lifting his chin at me.

'British.'

The other guy must be the stall owner. He's selling bottles of coke and sweets, matches and single cigarettes in a Tupperware box. Neither of the men look threatening.

'It is dangerous here,' says the first man, lifting his chin at Puerto La Cruz.

'Yes,' I say.

'You have no hotel?'

'Not yet.'

'Carnival.'

'Yes,' I say.

'*¿Todo bien?*' he asks Delores. She says something to him in her perfect Mexican Castilian. He laughs. BB and Carlos come up behind us.

'No room,' says BB.

'*Carnival,*' says the first guy.

'*Si, carnival,*' says the other guy.

'Yes,' says me.

'Next place?' asks Delores. I look at the map.

'Just up here on the left,' I say and we shoulder our packs again.

'Good luck,' says the guy.

'Thanks,' says me. Delores gives him a little wave and a brave smile. He blows her an almost paternal, entirely unsexual kiss.

The next place is full. So is the one after that. We don't meet any more friendly people, though we do meet some unfriendly people, and some quite scary people too. Eventually at about two-thirty, haggard and frayed, we give up on normal hotels and start asking in 'love' hotels.

Love hotels can be distinguished from other hotels because they only rent out their rooms per hour. They're generally seedy, noisy places, but at this time of night, what with the world turning into a twisted nativity scene and all, we have little choice.

The first three love hotels are all full. The fourth, thank the universe, has a double room, a grumpy night manageress with a tiny sliver of pity in her tired soul, cockroaches, squeaky bedsprings and two fold-up camping mattresses in a cupboard just for us. I have stayed in some fine hotels in my time but at this moment, in this town, I couldn't be happier. When the manageress leaves, closing the door behind her, the four of us look at each other. We're visibly vibrating with nervous energy. BB crosses his eyes. Carlos giggles. Delores squeaks and then we're all laughing our arses off, tension flowing out of us, fear rushing away, eyes brimming, helpless with hysterical relief.

'We're not dead,' says Carlos when he's got his breath back.

'No,' says BB, wiping his eyes on his sleeve, 'we are definitely not dead.'

'Sleep,' says me, fishing my toothbrush out of my bag.

'Sleep,' says Delores, pulling out her sleeping bag.

'Sleep,' say the boys. Sleep.

Puerto La Cruz is nothing fancy, just a few dirty blocks, cowboy-built, intersected by pock-marked lanes, filmy, stinking puddles and loud market stalls peddling cheap plastic 'Made in China' and fly-choked fish. Along the seafront, shops and cafés gleam only in comparison to the dull seediness to their rear. They line up like luncheon meat, sandwiched between the stink of tidal debris ahead and the trailing stench of decay and putrification behind. Four lanes of asthmatic traffic separate them from the ragged whitewashed palms and grimy yellow sand. Four lanes churning with beat-up pick-ups and ripped T-shirt barrow-boys, whistle-mouthed traffic cops swinging white nightsticks and urban cammo soldiers on 250 cc scramblers toting crowd-control Uzis. Like I said, Puerto La Cruz is nothing fancy.

I wake up groggy and unsettled. The adrenaline of last night spilled over into my dreams and gave me listless, uneven sleep. Slowly I remember waking up with Delores clamped around me, her face against my back, her skinny arms around my chest. I'd lain there for a while, enjoying her warmth, confused, wondering if she's asleep and imagining that I'm someone else, or awake and coming on to me. I'd snuggled back against her, wondering what to do with my erection, our sleeping bags cracking, the boys snoring on the floor, but she'd only held on tighter, skimming sexuality, her pubic bone pressed against the small of my back, until we slept again.

I open my eyes and look for her but her sleeping bag's empty now, the boys still snoring softly. I groan, drop my feet onto the floor and pad into the bathroom. The strip light clicks and fizzes and flashes on, flickering off mildewed tiles, whitewashed window panes, a dead cockroach under the sink. I wash quickly, get dressed in the dark, then I ease myself out of the door.

The street is unfamiliar in the morning light. Where danger had lurked in every corner there is just rotting rubbish, lizards sunning themselves and a scrawny dog sniffing at a pile of clamshells. I dodge puddles and dog shit, turn the corner at the end of the street and wander towards a café with tables on the pavement. Delores is sitting at one of them, camera in front of her, ashtray overwhelmed by Marlboro butts, nose in a book. I scrape a chair out and sit down opposite her. She puts down her book and smiles. I force a smile back. Then we both look across the road at the tattered palm trees and grimy beach, the line of oil tankers in the bay, the traffic in between. A waitress in a pink dress comes to our table and smiles at Delores. When she looks at me she doesn't smile.

'*Café, por favor,*' I say, too early for Spanish. 'Er... *negro, por favor.*'

She nods curtly and goes back inside. I reach over and take one of Delores' ciggies without asking, wondering if I should ask her about last night, but she beats me to it.

'I had a nightmare,' she says, taking a ciggie as well, 'it was about my boyfriend. I couldn't sleep afterwards. I've had about five coffees already.'

Boyfriend. I register the word but process it quickly and tell myself that it doesn't matter. Something shifts inside me though, something small. I sigh and flick ash onto the floor between my feet, watch as it blows away.

'Yeah,' I say, straightening up, 'I had a pretty rough night too.'

'Are the boys awake?' she asks.

'No,' I say, 'still snoring.'

The waitress brings my coffee and I stir in the sugar; the smell makes me feel better.

'An old Lebanese guy runs this place,' Delores says, her tone changing, shifting away from the word boyfriend. 'He was sitting out here with a bunch of old Jewish guys this morning. They invited me to sit with them and they bought me a coffee.'

I nod and force another smile, half turning in my chair to look into the café. I worry for a minute about Delores; she's so little and innocent looking, if it wasn't for her tattoos, dyed-black hair and dead-pan expression she'd look about fourteen.

'They were telling me about Chavez,' she goes on, blowing smoke into the wind, 'you know, the president? They were telling me he hates George Bush but he sells a million barrels of oil a day to America. All those tankers are going back to the States.'

I look out over the bay and wish I could speak Spanish, wish I'd sat around with a group of old men discussing politics over coffee.

'Did they say he's a good guy?' I ask.

'Who?'

'Chavez. I heard he was... different. There was a documentary...' My brain won't form proper sentences yet.

'Some of them liked him,' she says, 'others didn't. They

argued about it. They thought we were pretty funny for coming here for carnival.'

'Why?' I ask, but we both know the answer, you can smell it on the wind: with so many amazing beaches along the coast it does seem a bit funny to be in Puerto La Cruz. I drain my coffee and flick my cigarette into the gutter.

'Come on,' I say, pushing my seat back, 'let's go and wake the boys up.'

Later on that day we wander out of town along the beach looking for paradise, but the beach soon turns into wasteland and rusted iron ships, broken glass between the dry weeds. We skirt back inland and walk single-file beside the highway. The day is hot and dusty and there's nothing to look at but dead dogs and lizards.

When we get back Puerto La Cruz is warming up to carnival; an old Ferris wheel has been erected by the beach and there are cops and soldiers everywhere. BB, Carlos and I sit on a low wall with our backs to the sea and watch those fine Latina women go by, feeling left out and horny, our whiteness a barrier and an embarrassment. I feel like we're on display somehow. The Only Gringos In Town: a befreckled Swiss youth, a German Jesus and an uncomfortable looking Welshman. All lined up for your viewing pleasure, drunk, laughing, hollow with disappointment.

Delores sits quietly next to us chatting with a group of children who sell roses and sweets in little baskets, the skin on their bare feet dry and calloused, their grubby faces shining like they're talking to a princess. Soon we've all got more roses and sweets than we'll ever need and the kids all have ice creams and cheeky grins. Every time I look at Delores, surrounded by those glowing urchins, the word boyfriend pops back into my mind and the little change inside me pinches tighter and I have to remind myself that I don't fancy her, that there's something wrong somewhere, there must be; I can't like her. But it's not true.

That night, when I'm sure the boys are asleep, I try snuggling up to Delores again. At first she murmurs and wriggles closer to me, but then she wakes up a little more and senses that my motivation is twisted and horny and she goes cold and limp. I sigh and turn onto my back and wonder what the fuck it is I think I'm doing.

Why do I feel so seedy? Where has that feeling of purity and purpose gone? Why are we still in a flea-bitten love hotel in a third rate town?

The next morning we go looking for paradise again, this time in a cab, all of us dreaming of palm trees and white sands. Three miles west of town we are greeted by reality: the sun shining down wan and grey on a thousand empty deck chairs, sand like concrete dust and a soundsystem blasting dance music.

We'd all stayed behind in Caracas and waited for BB. We were all good people, our karma clear and clean. What have we done to deserve this? I suck it up and straighten my shoulders. Deal with it. We will have fun. That's what we're here for, fun.

I take off my shoes, grin at the others and they too shake the last of that paradise dream from themselves and grin as well. Fun!

But it's not fun. It's windy and ugly. The locals seem as tormented as we are, straining too hard to have a good time against the odds. We rent deck chairs for pennies and buy cold beers from a man with a wheelbarrow. Then we settle ourselves down to drown in dance music and forced gaiety. Pale and scatterbrained I sit myself down and drown in a Spanish phrasebook.

¿Donde esta me sanity?

At about twelve o'clock a huge army helicopter buzzes low

over the beach with its side door open and a big machine gun hanging out, grinning marine attached. Deck chairs and sun shades go flying and the waves are crushed flat, children scream and everyone gets a face full of sand. It hovers in front of us for a bit, then takes off down the coast causing merry mayhem as it goes. That is pretty much the highlight of our day.

An hour later a Venezuelan guy in Speedos comes and sits on a bit of driftwood next to us and starts staring at Delores.

'Are you okay?' I ask him, my hackles rising.

'Er... yes,' he says and shuffles a bit closer to me. 'Where are you from?'

'Wales,' I tell him, still a bit hostile. He nods like he doesn't know where it is.

'Are you enjoying yourselves?' he asks. We both look down the grey beach, at the grey day.

'Yes,' I say grimly. 'Yes, very much.'

'Good,' he says and he shuffles away from me slightly. We sit in silence for a minute and then I realise that I'm cheating myself by being hostile; there's so much I want to know and here's a guy who can tell me.

'Why are there so many soldiers and police about?' I ask.

'Chavez,' he answers. 'There are many people in Puerto La Cruz who oppose him.' He slides closer to me again and adds: 'Carnival.'

'Yes,' I say. 'Carnival'

Then I ask him about Chavez. I ask him about Venezuela. I ask him where paradise is. His name is Ramon, he works for Goodyear tyres, he lives in Valencia and the only reason he's in Puerto La Cruz is that the traffic was so bad he couldn't make it home. By now the others are sitting around us too, listening to Ramon, trying to ignore his wet Speedos. He says that Chavez is a bastard, that Venezuela is going to the dogs and that paradise is thirty miles to the east. Then the police start driving up and down the beach with loudspeakers telling everybody to go home. It's only about six o'clock. I ask Ramon why they want us to go home.

Ramon answers: 'Chavez.'

We walk back to his car with him and he offers us a ride. He has a very new, very shiny car. We spend a long time cleaning the dirty sand off our toes before getting in.

Back in Puerto La Cruz carnival is building up like a pressure cooker. The promenade is a standing wall of cars and Jeeps and distorted bass lines. We sit in the traffic for a while and Ramon turns to me.

'What are you doing tomorrow?' he asks.

'Getting away from Puerto La Cruz.'

In the back the others nod.

'Do you know where you're going?'

A Jeep full of screaming guys waving rum bottles mounts the pavement and ploughs slowly into a lamppost.

'No,' I say. The others shake their heads.

'Would you like to see some of the coast?' I turn round to look at the others. Carlos nods, but BB and Delores don't. Delores's eyes say 'I don't trust him. Did you see the way he stared at me?' BB's eyes say something similar. I'm feeling the same way but a lift down the coast in a flash car sounds good. Besides, we completely outnumber him.

'Can we think about it?' asks Delores.

'Sure,' says Ramon, adjusting the rear-view mirror to see her. 'I'll give you my number.'

Back at the love hotel the inevitable discussion takes place, but we're never far away from the fact that we need to get out of town and he's willing to give us a lift.

'He's pretty creepy though,' says Delores, flicking ash into an empty Sprite can.

'Never trust a man in Speedos,' I wag my finger at them.

'I used to wear Speedos,' says BB defensively.

'Me too,' says Carlos.

'But you don't any more,' says me, 'so I trust you.'

'What do you think he wants from us?' asks Delores.

'Maybe he's just being friendly.'

'Maybe', says me, 'maybe not. Listen. I think we should do it. It'll be better than the bus. We have to get out of this town. If he's a weirdo we can handle him. I don't think he's dangerous.'

Delores raises her eyebrows and shrugs, Carlos nods and BB shrugs too.

'Oh I dunno,' I lie back on the bed. 'Somebody else make the decision.'

The next morning we're sitting outside the old Lebanese guy's café at seven in the morning, our packs piled against the wall, waiting for Ramon to pick us up. The four of us are grumpy and hungover, frowning over our coffees, watching the crisp packets and beer cans blow along the beach, dogs munching chicken bones and candyfloss left over from last night. The wind smells of rotten seaweed and sewage, dead fish and hangovers.

A group of soldiers packing heavy assault rifles walks by. One of them says something as they pass us and the others laugh. I look down at my coffee and groan again inside. Like I said, Puerto La Cruz is nothing fancy.

6: Araguita

In a crackling-hot, jungle-choked valley of that country there is a tiny pueblo called Araguita. Up from the blue Caribbean Sea a little road winds its way through the grassy foothills and into the scrubby edges of the jungle. Then that dusty road turns slowly into a dusty track that winds further and further into the forest until the trees tower high overhead, letting in only a chink of golden sunlight here and there.

Little pueblos are scattered all the way up that road but as the track becomes dustier and smaller they get further and further apart. The track finally becomes nothing more than a broken path and, just when you think you can't drive any further, there is Araguita.

Little one-storey houses of breezeblock and concrete squat along the path that winds on up the valley into the jungle beside a noisy little stream. From the flat roof of every house rusted steel reinforcing rods point into the dappled canopy, ready for a second floor to be built when a little money can be made, or when a daughter becomes a mother, or a son a father.

Family is the most important aspect of life here. Cousins and brothers and sisters seem to live in every house. In the cool morning porches they sit laughing together, or they dance, rum-drunk and happy, deep into the night.

At carnival time the family crowds into the village bus with dogs and drums and cool boxes and tumbles down to the beach to picnic and dance and swim and laugh and drink La Brujita, 'the little witch', rum in green bottles full of roots and twigs and centipedes.

It is at the beach, one year, that the family find four pale gringos squatting in the sand, watching them with shy envy as the girls writhe laughing dances to the samba drums and the boys turn sandy back-flips.

After a time of exchanged glances and coy smiles Iago, the biggest and strongest of the cousins, swaggers over and offers his hand and a brimming glass of Cuba Libra to the gringos, who gratefully and self-consciously take both, and the family crowd around and one by one they offer their hands and smiles.

José, the fattest and friendliest of the fathers, ushers the baby-pink foreigners to the heart of the group: five cool boxes full of chicken and rice and ice-cold beer on which sit the plump mothers playing dominos and cackling merrily.

And so it was that the gringos met the family. They danced and sang and drank all day. Those who did not speak Spanish were assured by way of grins and drunken hugs that they were now part of the family and it made them all deeply happy.

Now it happened that the gringos had come to that particular beach because they had met a very different kind of Venezuelan the day before. This man was rich and well educated, he spoke fine English and drove a fast, air-conditioned car. He had befriended the group and, it being carnival, had offered to show them some of his country from the tinted windows of his fast car. Feeling fortunate indeed, they had accepted gratefully. As they passed through the barrios and little pueblos the rich man told them gravely about the bad deeds of President Chavez. How he favoured the lazy, dirty, frivolous common people over hard-working, serious upper classes. He told them how Chavez gave the poor money and food to vote for him. That he had tricked them into loving him. He told them that Chavez didn't really love the poor, only money and power. The gringos had listened and asked clever questions and nodded wisely. They understood how lazy and dangerous these poor people were, how they loved to rob and kidnap and murder. The gringos thought they understood the situation and the rich man was happy.

But now, on a beach near Araguita, they were fast becoming honorary members of just such a happy, murderous community, without hope or inclination of resistance. The gringos thought how different these people seemed from the description that the rich man had given them.

Perhaps the family are poor, they thought. *Perhaps they are frivolous. But that is not a crime. Most poor people are not poor because they are lazy. They are poor because they must be poor in order for the few rich people to be as rich as they like.*

The rich man stood in his Speedos under a palm tree nearby with his hands on his hips. It seemed that he was embarrassed to be with the family and that they were embarrassed to be with him. Though they were friendly towards each other their worlds where very far apart. So he stood underneath his palm tree looking unhappy while the gringo boys danced with the mothers and daughters and the gringo girl danced with the fathers and sons.

When the sun began to turn orange over the mountains it was time for the family to go home. The gringos had a drunken discussion with the rich man and the family and decided that they should all go to the village of Araguita to continue the fun. Two of the gringos climbed aboard the village bus and two followed after in the air-conditioned car. The rich man looked even more unhappy than he had before. Whether he feared for the safety of the foreigners, or whether he wanted them to see only his view of the country, none of them could tell.

When the family stopped in the town of Barcelona to watch the carnival parade the rich man made his excuses, said goodbye and sped off in his shiny car, back to his home in the affluent suburbs of Valencia, back to his safety, back to his security, whatever that might mean. The gringos were not sad to see him go. It had been strange for them to be the bridge between two worlds they did not really understand. They felt sure that they were now on the right side of the bridge and they all smiled and carried children on their shoulders and joined in with the bright and noisy parade.

On the bus back to Araguita everyone sang and laughed

but they were weary by now. The children fell asleep in the arms of the plump mothers and old José snored in the front seat. Up the bumpy track they went, up and up through the trees until they thought they could go no further and then, there was Araguita.

So it was for three days and nights the gringos became a part of village and family life. They climbed the dusty path through the jungle and swam in the cool waterfall pools. Iago taught them how to catch crayfish from under the rocks and little Edgar *'El Rata'* taught them how to play their card games. They drank ice-cold beer and shot the empty bottles to powder with ancient shotguns. They laughed as Uncle Herman, *'El Pollo'*, horsed around all arms and gangly legs and drunken comedian. They were dragged into water fights, late night dancing and football games. The plump mothers washed their dusty travel clothes and fed them good country food. The young, dark-eyed girls gave them nicknames and blew them giggling kisses.

It was good to be with the family. They worked hard and played hard. They looked after each other and never fought for long. One day the gringos asked José about President Chavez, they asked him if what the rich man said was true, and José said this:

'Hugo Chavez is a good man. He is a man who understands the people. He understands that if the majority of the people are happy then there will be peace and prosperity. This seems very simple to me but I don't think the leaders of the world understand it. Chavez is giving us a better life. We have more money, better schools and above all we are being listened to, we, the poor.

'But President Chavez is also a politician and he lives in a world of politics. He has a beautiful wife and fine clothes and fast cars even though he comes from a common pueblo himself. The people around him are corrupt, the police are corrupt, members of his government are corrupt. Perhaps even President Chavez himself is corrupt. This is bad but this is not the worst a man can be. If a man is mostly good and looks after his people well, so that his people have education, hospitals for the sick, food for the hungry and satellite television, then the people will love him and they will forgive him for being a little corrupt. It is better to be corrupt and good to your people like Chavez than being corrupt and bad to your people like George Bush. If I was Chavez I would have a fast car and a beautiful wife too!'

And then José's plump wife smacked him on the head for saying it and the conversation descended into another water fight.

All too soon it was time for the gringos to move on. They left the village in a haze of group photos and promises of return and letters and postcards.

Then they all piled into the back of Iago's jeep and tumbled down the dusty track towards the blue Caribbean sea.

Outside one of the pueblos along the way there stood a group of men dressed as women. They held a rope across the road and good-naturedly demanded coins from passing cars. The car ahead of the gringos was fast and expensive, the man driving it would not open his window so the children threw water balloons at him. Everyone was laughing but the fast car revved its engine and sped away whipping the rope out of the men's hands. As Iago drove by in his battered old Jeep he dropped a few coins into their bucket. That is how life is for the people of Venezuela.

The town seemed faceless and unwelcoming to the gringos when they finally arrived. Iago's smiling brown eyes filled them with deep love and affection as they said their last goodbyes. Then he drove away and the gringos sighed, alone again in Puerto La Cruz.

But Araguita will live on in their dreams and memories forever. They will live happily in the knowledge that in a cracking-hot, jungle-choked valley of that country, at the head of a dusty track, there will always be a bed, a good meal, a cold beer and a host of friends, arms open, eyes smiling, ready to welcome them home.

7: Choroni

I sit on my beach with my dog at my feet, on my soggy deck chair outside my tent.

My purple cactus-strewn hills march east through the mist and waves and shafts of milky morning sun whose hot light has reached the far western corner of the beach where a solitary, fat policeman in khaki shorts and vest does weak press-ups in the sand. To my right a lone old fisherman casts lasso-like a hand-line for spike-backed tiddlers which he'll fry up for breakfast. Technically, I suppose, the beach belongs to all three of us, but until the sun is well up and the beach folk arrive for a day of tanning and swimming, until old Antonio comes round to shin up the palm trees and drop coconuts thumping onto the sand to sell for peanuts to the city folk, until my new comrades rise yawning from their tents, until then, it is my beach.

The wind will pick up soon and the morning sun will force me shadewards. The posada at the head of the beach will begin its morning coffee and empanada distribution and I will wander over for sweet, black coffee and fried fish pasties.

First I'll sneak into the mangroves over there and try to

keep the mosquitoes off my arse while I make like a bear. Then I'll jump into the night-cooled sea and rattle my brain, shock my body awake and fill my sinuses with salt water, slide down the glassy waves as much like a fish as I can manage, never quite enough. But for now I am happy to be at my happiest, alone on my beach, quiet, with my dog at my feet, just the way I like it.

A few days after meeting the Araguita family Delores and I left BB and Carlos behind. We caught buses on opposite sides of a sticky tarmac road in Playa Colarada after hugging and exchanging fond goodbyes, then they headed east and we headed west.

Delores is travelling overland through Central America aiming to arrive back in Chicago in a couple of months and I have to stay relatively close to Caracas in order to meet my friend Lucy from the airport in a couple of weeks.

Lucy is an old friend from Brixton who has decided to come out and travel with me through South America. She's a bonny Scottish lass with an immense capacity for liquid refreshment and festivities. She also has a good friend in Caracas, called Clara, an artist, who's invited us to stay with her for a while.

So our bus came first and we waved goodbye to the boys and settled happily into that incredible stretch of coast between Cumana and Puerto La Cruz, where kids sell empanadas and areppas from baskets on their heads, where little houses of split bamboo and grass line the roadside, where palms and jungles collide and where little green islands wallow in pale blue bays.

Being on the road is less frightening and more addictive all the time, the feeling of freedom I get when I cast loose and drift into the future: no boundaries, no ties, no obligations, just me, Delores, the road and our fate.

That feeling is the reason I travel. Not so I can see the sights and tick off places on a map as other people do. I travel because it's my way of finding simplicity. All I have to think about from day to day are the bare necessities: food, bed and bus.

Though this sounds simple enough, those three little things can take a lot of organisation.

First food must be found which will not give me dysentery, Delhi belly, worms or amoebas. Next a bed must be found which contains the least possible parasites. It must be far enough off the floor so that nightly visitations from blood sucking maggots and giant centipedes can be avoided.

Then a mosquito net must be erected so I don't catch malaria, Japanese encephalitis, dengue fever, yellow fever, Saturday night fever or any number of other nasty diseases.

Then I have to find a bus which will take me to my carefully chosen destination. As often as not this is annoyingly and inexplicably not possible, Señor, so I have to make huge detours, wrestle with spare tyres or the lack of them, endure iron bouncy-castle-style comforts, non-existent roads, fellow passengers from a time before hygiene, and the odd night-time roadblock complete with sleepy Wil and young soldiers with assault rifles speaking too fast.

While under normal circumstances I perform most of the mundane tasks of life on auto-pilot, such luxury is not possible under harsh and foreign conditions, so I have to prioritise and simplify, thus forcing upon myself a more Zen-like existence.

Almost a week has passed since I set up camp and planted my Welsh flag on this beach. I know the approximate time from the position of the sun and its shadows. I know the dogs that live on the beach and they know me. Since I bribed them with fish skins and stale bread they bark at night if anyone comes too near my tent. I know that there are about three days till full moon and I know that I won't be here to see it. I know some of the villagers like me and others don't. Antonio, the coconut man, likes me because I help him drag his sacks of coconuts along the beach whenever we're going the same way. He climbs those trees so quickly you don't realise he's in his sixties till he gets to the bottom. I know the old fisherman likes me because he can sling his hand-line further than I can cast with my rod. He laughs his ragged old arse off at that. We don't talk much, we just wave at each other when I climb out of my tent in the morning and he giggles and makes ineffectual casting motions at me, standing in the shallows in nothing but a faded white shirt, white boxers and a straw hat, his little bowed legs all brown and sinuously fragile, white trousers rolled up on the sand beside his bait bucket.

I know the policeman doesn't like me. He told us to get rid of our fire one night after leaving us alone for days. Then he came back on the weekend and said he knew I'd been smoking weed. He sniffed me and searched me and grabbed me by the balls while his deputy stood by looking sinister and fingering the popper on his holster. Lucky the beach is a wonderful place to stash a little weed under half a coconut shell. Lucky I'm not so green any more and I played it polite and firm: '*Si Señor.*' '*No Señor.*' Lucky I'm so damn lucky or I might have found myself making a sizable donation to the local police force's booze and gun fund.

The sun reached my deckchair five minutes ago and mamma dog is getting restless in her sleep beside me. It's going to be a hot day, great blankets of mist are rising from the sand and I see the first people making their way down to the beach.

Soon my new French neighbours will be stirring as their

tents begin to cook and I'll wander down to the posada while the food is still crispy fresh.

Before I go I'll say this though: I can see that I am beginning to succeed in the first of my missions; I'm beginning to feel comfortable in situations I should naturally be uncomfortable with. Through recent times of hardship and loneliness I have lifted and carried myself forward and in this I have found peace.

Delores left a few days ago, on Valentine's Day, after sharing her sleeping bag with me for a week in my sandy little tent. We had a lovely time, just the two of us. I sang her songs and made her fires and she read to me in her little drunken kitten way. It was a lot like love, but we never even kissed. I suppose that makes no difference at all.

I miss her now but that's just how it goes. As soon as I stopped worrying about being alone, and let go of her, I felt empowered. The pair of us have miles to go, her north and I, eventually, south.

I can picture her on the road now: outrageously big boots and camera, her ragged little bag full of film and books, pale skin slowly turning brown, tattoos losing their stark abstraction.

Let the conformists conform and the meek be meek, for they will inherit only the conformity and meekness of the earth. The rest will be left to people like Delores.

It feels weird to be wearing clothes again. My skin feels chafed and smothered, my feet feel like they're blindfolded in socks and shoes. I have worn only a pair of shorts for so many days my body's over-heating with all this cloth covering me.

I feel sad to be leaving my beach. I have grown so tuned to its cycles, its tides and currents.

After Delores left I slept on the ground in my tent, with

nothing but a sandy sheet for warmth. I haven't shat in a toilet in weeks, haven't washed anywhere but the river. I've become almost entirely feral, catching my own fish from the market and foraging deep in the shady glens of the village shop for wild hot dogs and vegetables. It's funny how quickly we humans adapt to life without luxuries.

I'm on my way back to the city now, to re-adapt to a very different kind of survival. My pack feels twice as heavy as it was before I got here, what with all the sand I've collected. Everything I own is full of it.

It's early still. I got up just as it was getting light and packed while the dew was still down. I didn't see the fisherman, it must be his day off.

There's nobody about as I walk down the beach, but the posada is open so I drink a final coffee and explain to the giant of a woman stooped behind the counter that I'm off to Caracas. My Spanish is still terrible, but I'm more confident now and I can get my point across with a mixture of pointing, miming and broken vocabulary.

I cross the little bridge into the village. The fishing boats are still out, but by midday they'll all be moored here as usual, choking the stream mouth with their bright red fibreglass hulls. The palms along the water's edge are full of half-tame pelicans who eat the fish guts and heads that the fishermen throw them. The place would probably stink without them.

A few years ago Chavez set up a two-hundred-mile exclusion zone around the coast to stop factory ships cleaning out the fish stocks. Now the sea is full of big dorado and tuna and fishing villages like this one are thriving again.

I loved sitting and watching the fishermen at weigh in: small, compact men with huge stringy muscles, white grins and silver fish hooks in their ears. Everywhere there are piles of nets and polystyrene buoys with marker flags made out of old red 'Viva Chavez' banners from some past demonstration. I love that, turning a revolution won into a practical way of finding your fishing nets. *Chavez es el pueblo*, as the graffiti says.

I wander though the village and up to the bus stop near the school. A couple of times I've seen the school kids marching around the playground while one of the older boys drills them. It's Chavez's work again, keeping the populace trained and disciplined, ready.

People's sense of personal power is stronger here than in any other country I've been to. They know that they matter as individuals, in a political sense. They know that together they are strong, because they have proved it. When Chavez was kidnapped in 2002 in a failed coup attempt, when the former political elite tried to wrestle back their old power, the predominantly poor 'Chavistas' descended en masse on Caracas and demanded that he be reinstated. Thus the poor majority realised that they were not weak or insignificant, as poor people around the world are led to believe, and since then they have been preparing themselves to fight anyone who tries to reverse that realisation. It must have been a formidable sight to see the working class rise up. They are a happy, contented people now but it isn't hard to imagine them angry. No wonder the rich are hiding in their leafy suburbs.

I blend in enough by now not to be noticed. I don't have to ask the price of my fare or any other dumb gringo questions. I just nod when I see one of the fishermen I know, and wink at one of the girls from the village shop and that's about enough to make me as happy as a pig in shit. I am known. I am comfortable. I am a part of this!

The only way out of the village on public transport is in

old, brightly painted school buses with huge truck horns on their roofs. On the way here I thought the horns were just for show but then we started hurtling up the mountain roads at 60 m.p.h., around blind corners and switchbacks, one blast on the horn saved us from ever having to slow down.

I climb into the tiny bench seat and sit with my knees up by my chest and watch the jungle hurtle past. I've got a sweater ready this time because I know how cold it gets as the road weaves up from sea level and into the cool of the cloud forests on the mountain. The vegetation changes dramatically as we ascend, from the palms and huge, creeper draped trees at sea level to the darker, even bigger trees, tree-ferns and banks of mosses in the clouds. All along the road everything is covered in vegetation, even the telephone and electric wires sprout plants and weaver bird nests. Every so often a small waterfall crashes through the undergrowth and down towards the blue sea. The air smells like damp earth and fresh decay.

The bus is full today, full to bursting. There's a group of boys in the back with a box of small fish, which they keep throwing at a pack of giggling college girls. There's a bevy of fat mommas and skinny old men who chatter away unperturbed. There's a horde of school kids who put up a constant whirr of chatter. There's the three likely lads who drive the bus, pull the horn chain, play loud salsa and reggaeton, chat up the girls and generally look dapper in shirts, jeans, oiled hair and pirate earrings.

And then there's quiet old me.

I feel pretty pleased with myself all the way to Caracas. In Maracay I change buses like a pro, sit next to a pair of well dressed army officers who nod politely and watch the world and the slums go by with mild, un-squinting, un-gawping interest and when it's time, I move like a ninja through the subways and streets all the way back to the Nuestro Hotel.

It all looks so much smaller and less formidable than when I was first here. I smile at the old man like we're old friends and dazzle him with my linguistic abilities, which now stretch to being able to order a room and a beer. There's even enough left over for a bit of cheek for the sour-faced old bird who sits on her stool, surrounded by parrots, glaring at all the young couples who rent rooms by the hour.

I put my feet up on the plastic table on the balcony, kick back in my plastic chair, sip a cold Cynthia and smile pleasantly and wisely at all the scared, palefaced gringos who wander past, so full of fear, so in awe of Venezuela, Caracas – and me.

Later on, after failing to make any new friends because of my sizable ego and elevated self image, I swagger off to catch a tube and a bus to the airport to meet Lucy. The tube journey goes without a hitch, but when I get off at Gato Negro and climb the stairs to the street it starts raining. One look at the empty bus stops tells me the buses have stopped running and I realise that I'm not carrying enough money to get cabs to and from the airport. All of a sudden my cockiness is beginning to seem a little misplaced.

Still in my trusty, but busted, Green Flash, I wander the dark, glowering streets looking for a cab, feeling more and more alone and in danger as my feet get soggier and soggier. I hang around outside a phone stand where people pay a few pence to use mobile phones chained to a makeshift table, and try flagging a cab.

For some reason none of them want to stop for a soggy gringo tonight, they seem content to splash me and honk their horns instead. The crusty old man at the phone stand is squinting at me through the rain. I walk over to him and ask, in my best Venezuelan accent:

'*¿Donde esta el major place por un taxi del airporto?*'

'*¿Que?*' he asks, eyes narrowing.

I repeat myself, swapping some of the words around and making hand signals.

'*¿Que?*' he asks again.

'Taxi!' I yell. '*Airopuerto!*' I add a quiet, '*Por favor,*' when everyone turns to look at me.

'*¿Que?*' He asks a third time, cupping his ear.

I'm obviously talking to an idiot. I think and turn to one of the customers who is covering the mouthpiece of his phone and looking at me.

'*Discúlpame, amigo,*' I say, '*¿quiero un taxi por la airopuerto, donde esta el mejor place?*'

Fuck I wish I could remember the word for place or street or something, I think.

Soggy and pathetic by this point, I am hardly the shining, brown knight I'd pictured picking Lucy up from the airport. But, bless him, the guy puts down the phone and leads me to a different street where he dodges the flying puddles and puts me in a cab. I thank him and thank him and then settle down quietly in the taxi, watch the dripping barrios roll past and think about my day.

You got a bit too big for your boots there, young Willy, I tell myself, *and the universe took you down a peg or two. You're lucky you weren't mugged or raped as a lesson. However comfortable you get you should never be too cocky or self-confident. There is always more to learn.*

I arrive at the airport an hour late but Lucy still hasn't made it through immigration. I buy a coffee with the last of my money, amuse myself by looking for people who might be Lucy's mate Clara, and wonder how I'll make it back to

Caracas with no money if Lucy doesn't show up.

Twenty minutes later she comes through the double doors sporting that pale, drawn, London look and grinning fit to burst.

'Look at you, Willy', she says, holding me at arm's length, 'you've gone native!'

And then Clara's there too. Though I'd not spotted her before, she looks exactly how I'd imagined she'd look: corduroy jacket and jeans, insane black curls and a big, friendly smile.

'Wil,' says Lucy, 'this is Clara.'

'Clara,' she says, 'this is Wil.'

Mucho gusto, Clara, mucho gusto.

8: Merida

The mist clears and I wake up on a bus bound for Merida, a university town up in the Venezuelan Andes. When I went to sleep last night the bus was full of chattering children eating crisps and people wrapped up in pullovers and blankets. Now Lucy and I are the only passengers left. I don't remember everyone leaving.

It is a crappy bus, but that's all part of my new scheme: to travel on the lowest class of bus and therefore save myself money and, more importantly, save myself from the nightly freezing ritual common to most Venezuelan travellers of class. It's working too; I'm comfortable in my busted seat, well rested, and above all I am warm.

I slide open my mildewed window and light a ciggie, shuffling down in my seat so the driver won't see me in his mirror. I feel like a naughty kid.

Lucy is awake in the seat in front of me; I can see her through the gap in the chairs but she can't see me. She looks scared. I imagine it's because we're hurtling up some pretty alarming switchbacks at a pretty alarming speed. Lucy doesn't like heights. I don't ask her if she's okay though. I'm a bastard when I've just woken up, and I'm inexplicably grumpy with her already. She looks half-crazy, covered in old mascara.

It's been raining for days, weeks maybe. Roads and bridges have been washed out and all over Venezuela, according to TV news reports, landslips have destroyed villages, schools and churches. Land that was once rain forest is washed away because the roots holding it together have been burned and poisoned out to make room for grass and cattle.

There is at least one slip in every valley we pass though, here half a house, toilet hanging rudely over the red scar which was once a living room, there a whole hillside, trees and boulders, cars and all, piled massively in the swollen river below. Lucy is lost in stiff-sitting horror at these fresh chasms and dirty new cliffs, while I puff on naughty cigarettes and watch it all slide by in headphoned awe.

The bus driver doesn't seem to care about any of it. He's been driving for twelve hours straight by now and we've still got a couple of hours to go.

I stretch and yawn and put my faith once again in fate and forget the imminent danger. Lucy turns and sees that I'm awake and grins manically at me, knuckles white on the arm rest.

'Morning!' I yell happily at her. I'm such an arsehole.

We left Caracas after spending only a day with Clara because Lucy wanted to see some of the country. Personally I wanted to stay longer. I was intrigued by the small glimpse I got of real-life Caracas, and excited by what Clara said about the art and music scenes. I want to get deeper into this country instead of skimming the surface as a paleface tourist. But Lucy wanted her scenery, so Lucy gets her scenery: flirting with the edges of muddy chasms and hurtling through the weather-smashed valleys. I hope she's enjoying it.

When we get to town we find a hostel above a souvenir shop full of smelly alpaca and leather tat, and dump our packs in our windowless cupboard of a room.

An angry little woman owns and runs the place with her retarded side-kick – an odd little man who sits three inches away from the TV and interacts with garish soap operas as if he himself were a character.

I sit in a hammock and watch him over the top of my book. He gawps and gasps when the evil doctor turns out to be the huge breasted heroine's father. He shouts wordless warnings to the greased and handsome hero when the atmospheric music reaches a keyboard-demo climax and out steps the evil stepmother to do him some unspeakable mischief. The rest of the odd little man's time is spent sweeping the hallways, hanging out the frilly, pastel bedspreads and spying on the guests. I like him but I don't think he likes me much. My jovial interruptions of 'Buenos dias!' are usually met with blank terror and an inevitable scuttle for the safety of the laundry cupboard.

I am bored here already. I'm bored and I haven't got any weed. I'm bored and I haven't gotten laid for so long. Every complaint I have about life, however small, is blamed on the fact that I haven't gotten laid and I've got no weed. Life hurts with no sex and no weed.

Sometimes I'm quite content to play the abstaining monk. But not today. Not now. Not here. Not in bloody Merida. Outside our hostel is a small recreation area where young, fit, fitness-fiends do push-ups and pull-ups and squats and crunches and thrusts and squelches, watched intently by other appreciative fitness-fiends. All their pointless posturing and preening makes me sick...

I'm probably just redirecting emotions again. I'm probably just homesick. Probably insecure and lonely and homesick and bored...

... and horny.

I get like this sometimes. A hug and a cry usually cures me, but there are very few people I can hug and cry to and none of them are in Merida today. Lucy is someone I have hugged and cried to before, but our relationship seems to have changed since I left Brixton all those millennia ago...

So I buy a six-pack and sit dejectedly in the leafy little plaza surrounded by couples kissing and cuddling on park benches. The air is full of birdsong and the soft murmurs of Latin love. A pair of coppers stand by the fountain watching me, watching my beers disappear, watching my sulky annoyance turn into drunken listlessness. I don't have to be doing this to myself. I could pull myself together, but right now this is all I want to do; wallow in self pity and pour surly scorn upon the world.

9: The Old Country

The air is thinner already, breath seems harder fought just sitting on the bus. For hours now we've wound our way upwards through ancient hill country still turned by ox and hand-plough. The passengers travelling from village to village could be from any decade, so rare are glimpses of modern living: the same old Stetsons that they've worn for generations, the same old leather jackets and jeans, the same old dusty cowboy boots. They kiss their crucifixes and cross themselves when they sit down, nod to each other and smile with their black eyes, eyes set in such weather beaten faces, such wind and sun burned skin.

Lucy and I sit quietly and smile respectfully, fully aware that these people are deeper than we are, that these are real people somehow. All the complaining I've done lately now seems like the whinging of a spoiled child. These people are of rock and stone, of earth and hardship and smoky kitchen fires, of horny calloused hands, of oil lamps and burros and God. Perhaps the only place He still exists is with people like these. We are quietened and soothed by their company, and when the bus stops in the little village with the stone church we are more relaxed with each other.

It's colder up here at about 3,500 metres above sea level. Lucy hurt her back so I'm carrying enough food, clothes, shelter, water, med kit, cooking gear, fishing gear and luxuries for three nights, even though we only plan to be out for one. It's all very heavy. I have never been at high altitude before and I've been smoking cigarettes for weeks and not doing much exercise. We only have one sleeping bag. Lucy is an asthmatic.

We have a map which we managed to copy from a young tour guide we befriended in Merida. We'd popped into the shop to see if we could rent sleeping bags and mats and asked him if he could recommend anywhere we could walk without bumping into other tourists. He got all excited and told us that he was from a village in the mountains accessible only by mule track. He told us that it was as remote as we were likely to get without horses, gave us lengthy directions and family addresses and told us to look out for mountain lions.

The map is a military OS with a scale so small that it is relatively useless, but it feels good to have one anyway: at least we can check our altitude.

I run through a final gear check while Lucy walks to the posada to ask which path we should take out of the village, and, amid the amused smiles of interested locals, we're away.

The first few hundred metres are the worst. Before our

bodies get warmed up, before our minds can comprehend that there really is so little oxygen getting to our blood, before the constant headache and light-headedness becomes normal.

Ten minutes in and Lucy is dying already. I stop and talk her through what's happening and how it will get easier and we share a chocolate bar to get our blood sugar up. Her face is beetroot-red and she's puffing like a steam train. I'm carrying my own body weight in gear and every time I look at the miles of incline ahead I want to cry, but I tell myself it's my own fault for smoking so much and start counting baby steps and try to get a rhythm.

Imagine if you sprinted as far as you possibly could, then jumped up and down on the spot, singing at the top of your voice: that is what every small step feels like when you're not used to high altitude. Lungs burn, eyes bulge and temples throb. It's no fun.

But soon we toughen up. Soon we're above the village and looking back at mile upon mile of hazy, washed-out green hills, craggy, black rock mountains and ravens. Soon the road is behind us and we're in a land forgotten by time and technology and every breath hurts, but that's okay because yonder farmer waves a lazy salute from his bull-plough and an eagle soars above us, and we're used to the pain by now and there's our path winding on and on into the mountains, and ain't you glad we came? And then we're up and off again and goddamithurts what the fuck are we doing here? We must be crazy and left... left... left... right... left... and head down and pump those legs slowly, slowly, rhythm going now and push and push and breathe, but don't think about breathing because when you do you can't breathe so don't think about it and push and pump those legs and left... right... left... and collapse once more and look about and ohmygoditsbeautiful but fuck me I'm gonna pass out...

... and on and on and up and up. Slowly and steadily, past potato pickers on impossibly angled fields, past ancient roundhouses and stone corrals, past waterfalls and sunlight dancing in frigid, crystal water.

In a pleasant green valley, the last flat ground before the mountains soar up and majestically away, we break off from the path, eyes wide for snakes, and flop down near the stream for lunch. We collected potatoes dropped by the farmers on the way up; I light a fire with tinder-dry scrub wood and fry them with ham and garlic and eat them on squashed French bread with black coffee cooked in a tin can.

The sun warms us and we lie back out of the wind and listen to the trout rising for flies and watch the vultures circle high above us and the horses grazing upstream.

It is early afternoon by the time we start again and we're so tired and relaxed that we decide that it would be safest to pitch camp in the head of the valley and walk over the pass to the village tomorrow. We take our time pitching camp and collecting wood and cooking dinner, the pair of us content in our work even though every movement is a chore and every time we stand up our hearts race and our vision blacks out.

As soon as the sun sets the temperature drops dramatically but we've both got thermals and layers and there's lots of firewood so we sit in the flickering light and drink sweet coffee and gaze up at the stars. I can honestly say I've never seen so many, so bright, so clearly, in my life. It's as if space is not black at all but alive and bulging in every direction with twinkling light. We watch a UFO move around in slow triangles above us in the bowl of the plough and talk about the size of infinity until it hurts.

That night, I can just as honestly say, I got as cold as I ever want to get. With the sleeping bag over both of us and all our clothes on we thought we'd be okay. When the water bottle froze next to my head I knew we were in trouble. I slept five minutes at a time and shivered even then. It was miserable. I wanted to sleep so much after the day's climb, but I knew that if I slept too deeply I probably wouldn't wake up. Every time I dozed I'd have nightmares about people sitting on my chest or smothering me. The blood banged in my ears and I just couldn't get a rhythm in my breathing; every time it slowed down I'd run out of oxygen and end up gasping for breath and hyperventilating.

Lucy and I were wedged as close together as we could get but the ground was so cold we could only stay a few minutes on one side before our shoulders, hips and ribcages grew numb, then we'd wake each other up turning over and open cracks of poisonously cold air in our covers and have to start the warming process all over again.

Eventually, covered in all our gear, pack and all, I managed to get enough warmth to sleep for a full half hour.

I dreamt again, with incredible lucidity, but this time it wasn't an oxygen nightmare, this time I was in the oak wood above my home in Wales walking barefoot through the bracken, and when I woke up again I felt weirdly calm and comfortable.

I knew then that I had to get up, leave the sleeping bag to Lucy, light a fire and keep myself alive till dawn.

So in the dark with the night noises all around me I gather wood, shivering wildly. Periodically I jump up and down and flap my arms to get the circulation going.

The sky is draining light blue to the east by the time I get a decent fire going, my hands shaking like an alcoholic with Parkinson's. I squat on the pebbled stream bank, my hands inches from the flames, and watch, trancelike, the colours appear around me, deep blues and greys in the sky revealing the mountain shapes slowly in monotone, and as the east turns red and purple, the yellow and orange of the grasses and rocks become clearer until the sky is a massive, silken blanket of soft blue and indigo and the craggy peaks glow purple and the dead grass on the lower slopes burns yellow. Then the sun touches the peak high up behind me and I know that it will be a long time before the sun reaches the valley floor and me.

I raise my weary, gasping self and make a can of coffee, fumbling with the knots in the plastic bag and burning my frozen fingers over and over again and then burning my mouth with the sweet, steaming liquid as it goes down, but ahhh it's so good. It's like life itself flowing into me and I finish it before it's cool enough to drink and make another.

For three-quarters of an hour I sit and watch the sunlight move down the mountainside towards me, stoking my fire, making and drinking coffee after coffee, jumping about periodically and rubbing myself vigorously all over. I must be quite a sight for the cougars, vultures, owls and goats.

And then it hits me, coming low and fast across the valley floor BANG! Hits me, legs spread, arms spread, head back, shouting as devoutly as any sun worshipping Inca, as sweet as any spring-goaded Snowdrop-pop. Mighty Pacha Mama. That vast and glorious ball of hydrogen. That incredible chemical reaction in the sky throwing cosmic warmth down on me at a mighty 186,000 miles per second. Not only do I revolve around you but I fucking love you! Hallelujah! The night is over, the cursed absence of solar energy has ended and *I am alive*!

Seconds later I start sweating. Seconds later I have forgotten almost entirely the feelings of desperation and the depth of suffering to which I was married before the sun came up. Seconds later I am cursing myself for wearing too many layers and I'm stripped to my long johns, boots and a sweaty sweater. Seconds later I am bringing hot-coffee-in-bed to a surprisingly well slept Lucy and jabbering and jittering away about goats and ice and hypothermia and too much coffee.

We are ungrateful creatures, we humans. We pray and whine for deliverance and as soon as it is delivered we skip off down the road waving a half-hearted thanks and pay the whole thing no more mind. And so it is today. We eat breakfast, strike camp, vow never, ever to camp at high altitude without proper gear again, stash the pack and saunter off, albeit a little wheezily, up the winding mule track which leads to the pass.

It's all routine from there really. Lucy scrambles up, eyes closed, reeling with vertigo but determined to make it with a little light encouragement from me. 'Stop being such a fucking pussy and get the fuck up that mountain!' If it's how I talk to myself and get things done why shouldn't it work for other people?

Politely, in lilting Glaswegian, Lucy tells me to go on ahead and go fuck myself and catches me up at the pass, a mere 4.6 kilometres above sea level.

The land is spread out all around us, distant snow-capped peaks and golden hills, deep blue lakes and wooded valleys. Ahead and below us is the village we set out for. It's perched on the slopes of a great peak, looking deceptively close. But, like all true adventurers, we decide that the whole thing is way too much trouble and scuttle back down the way we came. Happy to leave cold mountains and oxygen-starved hardship behind in favour of hot showers, beds, beers and oxygen, sweet oxygen.

It turns out that we had walked a lot further than we'd imagined on that first day, heads down and going steady. The country around us seems so unfamiliar I keep thinking we're lost.

We eventually arrive back in the little village with the stone church, and flop down on the roadside with a six-pack from the posada and take off our boots. Our swollen, white feet are covered in blisters and we compare aches and pains and smoke and chat to a pair of inbred-looking local kids on their bikes. They don't know much about much, but they tell us which bus is ours and when we run to catch it Lucy kicks the curb barefooted and splits her big toe neatly in two.

And so onto that respectful, Christian bus we clatter, stinking, bleeding and dragging pack and beers and boots. I dig out my med kit, wedge myself in the aisle and clean and dress Lucy's bleeding toe. The locals gather around and Lucy tells them, 'It's fine, he's a doctor,' and they all nod soberly and pat me on the shoulder and congratulate me on what a fine physician I am.

So back I sit in my lofty position as dirty-nailed village witch-doctor and drink my beer and contentedly watch the world and its donkeys slide by.

'If you can't get laid…' a man once said, 'get up in them hills and get cold and breathless… cold and breathless.'

10: Back to Caracas

It is early morning by the time we arrive back in Caracas. Lucy and I are grumpy. As we leave the bus station and weave our way through the crowds to the underground we don't speak more than a few words.

It was not meant to be like this of course. We're meant to get on as well as we did in Brixton. We aren't meant to be at each other's throats, but we are, and no matter how mature and rational we try to be we still annoy and alienate each other. Sometimes people are just not meant to be together, even old friends. Sometimes it's wiser to call it a day and go in different directions than stick it out and lose each other entirely.

I know she's thinking the same thing; we haven't discussed it but it hangs between us, wet and stringy. The past is irrelevant, we are connected now only by our mutual need to break our connection, to go our separate ways.

So after we arrive back at Clara's and shower and sit for a while under a blanket of grey moodiness, Lucy, to my surprise and admiration, says:

'I might go to Colombia.'

There is a silence. Clara can sense the tension between us. Lucy's waiting for me to say something but I don't know what to say. I want to tell her to go, but I don't want to hurt her feelings by seeming too keen. So I sit in silence. It is Clara who speaks first.

'It is very dangerous to go alone,' she says, looking down at her glass of wine.

'I can handle that,' Lucy says dismissively. She can too.

'How long would you go for?' I ask her.

'Maybe a month.' Then she looks at me and says, as an attempt at reconciliation, 'I'll meet you in Peru.'

'That'd be nice,' I say, being pleasant to her for the first time in a while.

'I just feel like I have to go, now that I'm so close,' Lucy goes on. 'It'd be stupid not to.'

I open my mouth to say something defensive about why I'm not going, but then I shut it again.

'What will you do if she goes?' Clara asks me, later, when we're alone.

'I might stay in Caracas for a couple of days,' I say and then I think: *I have to ask, I'd be stupid not to.*

'Can I stay with you, Clara?' My voice sounds dumb when I say it. 'I'd love to check out some music and art and...' and I trail off.

Clara looks at me. I can tell she's thinking about Lucy,

wondering whether it would be disloyal. Then she seems to make her mind up.

'Of course you can stay here, Wil,' she says and ruffles my hair like a big sister. 'I'm quite busy but I'd love to show you my city.'

I wander back indoors where Lucy's doing the last of her packing.

'Are you sure about this?' I ask her, handing her a pair of flip-flops. She looks up and draws in a long breath.

'Yes,' she says, exhales. 'Yes I am.'

But I can tell by the way she looks away quickly that she's scared and that makes me feel bad. I feel responsible. I hope nothing bad happens to her.

'You'll be fine,' I say as convincingly as I can. 'You'll be fine.'

And I feel guilty, even though I know we'd end up hating each other if we stayed together much longer, I still feel guilty.

11: 'Asian Success Week'

Contrasting starkly with the sprawling, haphazard barrios that make up most of suburban Caracas, Alto Prado, Clara's neighbourhood, is ordered, affluent and clean. There is a sterile sense of safety; every house hides behind high walls and security fences while noisy dogs do their best to make passers-by feel unwelcome.

They are scared, these people, scared of uprisings, scared of Chavez, scared of the armed and righteous poor. Secretly though, I feel they'd welcome a civil war, a chance to use their oiled and polished machine guns, a chance to see whether or not there is a vicious bite behind their dog's vicious bark.

I don't feel entirely comfortable here. It all seems a bit

unrealistic and naïve. There is no sense of community, no borrowing of sugar, no chatting over the razor-wired garden fence, no love.

This morning, as usual, I'm drinking coffee in the sun outside Clara's room. Beside me, in a cage full of rotting fruit, is a parrot. As usual the parrot woke me up, screaming 'Claaara! Claaara!', monotonously. As usual old Papa Muerte, the least vicious and most pathetic of the neighbourhood dogs, is trying to lick my face, long tentacles of saliva drooping from his lumpy pink jowls.

Clara lives in a converted garage connected to her dad's house. He often pops round to check up on his thirty-six-year-old daughter; this sends her into fits of rage.

'Why is he always here? I'm a grown woman. Why does he keep being so nosy?'

I like Clara's dad. His brothers, Clara's uncles, were guerrillas back in the seventies and eighties when the totalitarian state was at its strongest. They still live in their camp in the jungle. Clara's dad farms coffee on a plot nearby. This morning, as usual, I am drinking his coffee. Black. Two sugars.

Clara emerges behind me, bleary, brown-eyed and tousled. There was an article in the paper about her yesterday, 'a portrait of the artist'. She is a very successful sculptress in Venezuela.

'Shall we esmoke a joint, Weel?'

She is also a very successful pot head.

'Sure,' I grin. 'Why not, Claret?'

We sit about in the little square of concrete and aloe vera plants that is her garden. It smells powerfully of sun-dried dog shit and piss. Most mornings Clara's dad hoses it down obtrusively. Most mornings Clara complains:

'Why does he have to do that now? Why is he in my espace again?'

There's a big turd drying unobtrusively next to a plant pot.

Clara's dad must have gone to the coffee farm this morning.

We pass the short, pure joint between us. It gets a bit soggy towards the end. It's only 8:30 a.m. and I'm blazed as a bastard again. This is how I immerse myself in foreign cultures: I wake and bake.

For the rest of the day Clara and I wander Caracas. She has errands to run and I tag along. The bus down to the city plays soothing soft rock. I sing along to 'Hotel California'. I hate the Eagles but it's in English, look everyone it's in English!

Caracas is a crazy city. Half finished flyovers and tower blocks rot and rust like huge broken tombstones, ugly memorabilia from the economic handover.

Political graffiti cover the grubby walls proclaiming to passers-by '*Chavez es el pueblo*', and '*Abra los cajas*'. Here and there are little stencils of Che Guevara, Chavez as an angel, Chavez as the devil. The whole country, it seems, is divided between those who love Chavez and those who hate him. I'm beginning to lean towards the loving side. Clara does. Her mother, on the other hand, hates him, her father loves him. The rich are supposed to hate him, but in every well-off household we visit there is the same passionate conflict between those who love him and those who hate him. While the English make small talk about the weather, the Venezuelans chat about politics. Everyone is very passionate about it. I am a bit lost to be perfectly honest, but I like Chavez and his modern socialism, if only for the fact that he so openly badgers George Dubya and his Neo-Con cronies. I watched a bit of Alò Presedente, Chavez's seven hour Sunday morning 'address to the nation'. He was asking members of his cabinet if they'd marry Condoleezza Rice. The ministers all took turns to make faces and say exaggerated 'No's. Chavez nodded wisely, turned to camera and said:

'You see Condi, no one is going to marry you unless you start making some changes to yourself. You make yourself very undesirable.'

I like Chavez for that, the cheeky, chauvinistic bugger.

Clara shows me around the art school where she studied. It's a great grey cube of concrete that hunkers down in front of a mass of housing projects. It was from those housing projects, Clara says, that the first wave of protestors came when Chavez was kidnapped. What the school lacks in appearance it makes up for in personality. There is a crackle of creativity in the air, the students seem almost militant in their concentration and productivity and there's a definite feeling that 'things are happening' here.

That night we go to a party in an apartment block in downtown Caracas, a celebration of the launch of Clara's friend Fredo's exhibition.

It is a strange party yet, to my mind, a wholly familiar one. Strange that it should be in Caracas, but familiar in that I've been to it a hundred times before.

There is a lot of cocaine floating about in little polythene bags wrapped shut with white cotton. That is an important fact. There is a constant and ornery queue for the bathroom. That is to be expected. There is loud music and plastic glasses, fashion, money and a cauldron of rum-punch that looks like it might be a trap.

But there is no beer. So Nacho, a tubby friend of Clara's who lived in South London for a few years, and I run around the corner to get some. As the old lady at the counter slides the beers into brown paper bags we talk about how similar the party is to some jumped-up Shoreditch arty-party, how it has the same tower-block industrial-kitsch feel to it, the same cutting-edge fashion clones in the same trucker caps and tight jeans, the same coke fetish that lends to the party the same insincerity and bullshit, the same tired, unspoken, double-negative mantra:

I wouldn't be here if it wasn't for coke, I wouldn't be like this if it wasn't for coke, I would be shy if it wasn't for coke, I wouldn't have said that if it wasn't for coke.

We laugh all the way back to the apartment about these sad fucks who can't handle life without a line and in the lift we kill each other about how these cool rich kid are clones of the same preposterous, foundationless, conforming chameleons in every city, on every continent worldwide.

And as we walk in the front door we meet those same people with smiles and cheers. Fredo charges over, sporting a Grizzly Adams and armfuls of tattoos, demands a beer and drags us into the bathroom, ushers out the previous, snuffling occupants and produces a bag like a tupping-ram's testicles. He talks in too-fast Caracas slang, S's dropped and unintelligible to me and he racks up big, white lines the size of spare ribs on the plastic cistern. Then he rolls proud and beautiful Simon Bolivar into a tube and we take turns to stick him up our noses, thanking each other politely, noticing Fredo's neck veins bulge and his left eye twitch. Then we burst out and into the party again to join the clones, and become clones ourselves, clones of a worldwide social movement going nowhere, to slowly start that merry mantra for ourselves: *I wouldn't be like this if it wasn't for coke...*

The party peaks and troughs, peaks and troughs, as if the moon were pulling people tidal ways. Beer can and plastic cup flotsam fills the corners. The marooned sit in groups on the floor and talk in beautifully expressive Castilian.

I am smiling now. Smiling at it all.

Fredo's girlfriend, a tall Venezuelan/Thai called Yon, is giving me a guided tour of the paintings; little low-brow canvasses of cats on motorbikes and penguins in pyjamas. She's making up a spoof artist's commentary on each piece. I haven't really talked to her before even though I've been introduced to her a couple of times over the past few weeks. Other people's sexy girlfriends are like that for me: better to steer clear and keep my life an easy one.

Her English is excellent and she's smart and beautiful. We laugh together, and I don't really love Fredo that much so I talk to his girlfriend and watch him out of the corner of my eye and politely piss him off. I'm not a vindictive person but the guy's an egomaniac, someone has to take him down a peg or two.

I wouldn't have said that if it wasn't for coke

Then I'm drifting around by myself again and smiling and confident, but not quite part of it all, buzzing and whooping on the inside and cool and pleasant on the outside, like summer morning wrapping-paper full of bees, like bees gift-wrapped in a summer morning.

I'm chatting to a man about London, half listening: he went there for a week once and... em... whatsitcalled... when in walks Maiko Mao.

Oh, it's one of those moments. One of those moments when your eyes meet someone else's and you immediately feel like you should be saying hello and finding out how that person is, even though you have no idea *who* that person is. It's one of those moments from a soft rock ballad or an R&B slowjam, only without the basic evil associated with those genres.

She's small and lovely looking, is Maiko Mao. She's Asian/Latina, with long, healthy black hair down to her cute little butt. Of course I don't know she's called Maiko Mao yet but it's such an apt and lovely little name, the way it rolls off the tongue in baby-talk syllables, we'll use it before its time anyway.

I stand in the corridor out of the way but in her way,

positioning myself to collide with her future without really noticing what I'm doing, watching her, half smiling and confident and '*I would be shy if it wasn't...*' but it *is*, so here I wait and watch and catch her eye again and make a face and she laughs and covers her mouth with her hand like a good Japanese girl. She says hello to someone else and watches me again and slowly moves through the hellos until she's looking up at me with a quizzical little face of olive skin and cat's eyes and perfect, pursed lips.

'Hello, I'm Wil.'

And in my head it sounds like, 'Hello, I'm Johnny Cash.'

Cocaine. The only time I feel comparable to the man in black is when I'm dusting my insides with white. But it works wonders sometimes, that white bravery, to take away your needless fear for an hour or two, and sit you down on the floor among the seaweed and shells of the apartment and talk and laugh and trail off the laugh with a sigh and a silence and a look in each others eyes. Ah, young love.

She loves the Welsh, does Maiko Mao, having met a Welshman once who was a legend, as they say. She asks what am I doing here and I wax lyrical about my travels, and she laughs at me and I like her for it, and we laugh and sigh and give each other where-have-you-been eyes.

It's all quite sickly and sticky really, but I haven't been to the cake shop for so long that I'm like a fat kid with a filling and a fiver.

It's nice though. We exchange numbers and she leaves early and I feel like a gangster and a pimp, and flop down next to Clara for my dig in the ribs, 'Who's that girl, Weel?', and winks from the others, and I smile bashful and play shy and lap it up.

And then it's cries of: 'let's quit this dying beach party and head out to sea,' because the night is young, because the drug is young in our veins. So it's out we pour into those dangerous, balmy streets awash with the sweet smell of lilacs and drains and we hail old Cadillac taxis and bounce and roar away, talking loud and fast. My face pressed up against the cool glass watching the midnight with delicious fear and admiration.

It is shadow and desperation and toughness, the midnight, and then it's a screeching stop and the bass notes of salsa and lights flashing in the alley and hugs for Clara from the doormen and smiles and handshakes for the rest of us, and the usual 'this is my gringo brother Weel' and into the noise and the light.

El Mani exists in an antiquated world of its own, a world where the laws of time are lax, a world where music is time and music is adlibbed so time is freestyle. A couple from the 1920s dance, hips thrust together, faces set in stiff-necked, haughty concentration, feet stamping and weaving in perfect time. Next to them dance a couple from our time, grinning but no less sophisticated, no less fluid, no less a part of this place and time.

We make an island for ourselves beside the small wooden stage and order bottles of rum and mixers from the uniformed waiter and take turns escorting white, cotton-tied bags and Simon Bolivar to the toilet.

Then the band begins. Seven Latinos and Morenos in linen and pomade. Seven instruments. Seven suave smiles. The vibraphone leads, the bassist follows and then the drums attack, a tight chicken strut break, a cocky chest puff rhythm, and then the sax and trombone and trumpet lean in and squawk and lean out, lean in and squawk and lean out and they're away, flying and snatching and thumping a beat out of these old sweat-dark floorboards from which a hundred thousand beats have been pounded before. And now, hand-on-heart, hat-low, eyes-closed, the singer summons a portal from which upon us gush a hundred lifetimes of pain and love and poverty, and the chickens scrabble in the dust and the moon shines down on the burros tied in the plaza and the gypsy's daughter takes your hand in the darkness and you smell her hair and she is warm and she smells so good and you dance and dance like love itself until the cockerel crows from the barnyard and all around is dust.

Memory sleeps and wakes and I'm opening my eyes and the sun is well up. Everything hurts. My mouth feels like a swollen sandpaper pouch full of wasabi. Light reflected off the world attacks me viciously, the phone is ringing next to my head and the parrot is screaming 'Claaaara! Claaaara!' from the yard but Clara's not up yet and it's all too much.

So I bury my head again and let it ring, let it scream and let it shine because none of them are for me. Not now. Not yet.

'Phone for you, fucking Weel!' The Claret is not happy. I protest that no one knows me here, how could it be for me? But it's already too late and Clara has gone back to bed. I crawl to the phone and groan hello as a chirpy Maiko Mao wishes me a very good morning and wonders whether I'd like to take her to lunch. That fat kid from the cake shop is at the door again, and no matter how hungover I am, he's not taking no for an answer.

In half an hour I'm up and crouching in the shower, moaning long, wordless moans to myself, washing as much of the filth out of my brain as I possibly can. With clean clothes and sunglasses on I no longer feel like I might die, instead I settle into feeling terrible and slither to the bus stop and try as hard as I can to block out soft rock bus music through gritted teeth and a spinning world.

We arranged to meet outside the Jehovah's Witness church in Chacaito. It used to be a cinema years ago but now, instead of ushers, young men and women in bad suits, shiny shoes and name tags paw and grab at passers-by eager that they too should witness Jehovah.

Maiko Mao is late so I buy a chocolate milk and sit down heavily on the old cinema steps and watch the meek shepherd the weak. Soon they decide that I too should be shepherded, but I put their worrying minds to rest by explaining that I follow only the dark one himself and that inviting me inside would be a bad idea. They're just getting the point when Maiko shows up. She's different now that I'm not wasted. She's lovely and elfin and bouncing all over the place with happy elfin energy. I stand there grinning at her over the insistent Witness's shoulder, then she takes my hand and we just walk away and my hangover seems to turn inside-out and life is warm and friendly again and I don't really worship the dark one.

What follows is a montage of soft-focus, happy memories which fade mistily in and out of each other while soft rock plays in the background. The colours in these memories are pastel pinks, purples, oranges and blues. Our hair is big. We laugh over lunch and exchange happy life and family stories and everyone is happy. We give happy money to a happy bum and stroll in the happy park and laugh some more, our perfect teeth are very white and they glint in the sun. At weak orange sunset we lie in each other's arms in the soft grass and kiss and wonder at loneliness vanished and the sadness of parting and I stroke her hair and we are happy.

Then we are wishing each other a sweet goodnight outside her gated apartment block and everything fades to black as I wave goodbye from the window of a taxi...*

(Note how selective editing and genius post-production has erased or hidden all evidence of crushed boners and nut-rearranging in the park. All traces of blue-ball and 'I still live with my parents, I'd love you to come up but they wouldn't like

73

it,' have been skilfully eradicated. As has *'It's okay, I don't mind. Let's hang out again soon. I had a great day,'* said politely, though insincerely. The absence of these events need never be noticed. Nor should the absence of perfect teeth, big, eighties hair, or sincerity.)

The moving picture show fades into a tired shot of me in the back of a crusty cab once again sliding through the streets of night-time Caracas. Romance has gone the way of yesterday's white stuff and my soppy endorphins can no longer bear to make me happy. Earlier lust and passion has soured into a headache and a bad mood, my hangover has reinvented itself as something new and vile.

Clara is waiting outside the opening night of Caracas's newest gay club. I am 'I can't be bothered' written in posture and expression, but she slaps me on the back and leads me past more friendly door staff into a cramped basement full of smoke and house music and drag queens tottering on too-high heels.

I find myself a White Russian and a couch and I smile at people I know and assure the concerned that I'm just having a little rest, I'm perfectly fine. But I'm obviously too much of a downer for this gay little scene so into my palm is pressed a cotton-wrapped bag of polythene and hydrochloric acid, among other things, and Simon Bolivar and I slip once again into the bathroom to beast the serotonin mill into hyper action.

As the party gets more interesting or I get more interested, I begin to enjoy myself. Clara is in the middle of a girls-night-out dancing session with garishly dressed-up friends to whom I smile encouragements and occasionally raise a toast. Out of that near-hysterical group pops a beautifully dressed Yon brandishing a White Russian at me.

How did she know I was drinking that? I wonder. *Did she ask the barman? Has she been spying on me?*

She sits down next to me and it's comfy and relaxed and

we talk. She has to shout and lean into me to be heard and I do the same and it's intimate and I can smell her perfume and see down her long, lovely back. But I've already had one montage scene today, another one would just be greedy, so I tell Yon about my day, I tell her how innocent it all felt with Maiko. I tell her how I lost my innocence so long ago that it makes me feel insincere to be so mushy and romantic. I shout all that into her ear and it makes me feel better and she smiles at me and I have to remind myself again that people in other people's girlfriends shouldn't throw stones. I shuffle an inch away from her on the couch but she sees what I'm thinking and she smiles again.

Later on we're drunk and she's telling me how unhappy she is in her relationship. I play the strong, understanding, big brother and hold her hand. Then she leans in and kisses me and I reluctantly push her away and tell her that it's a bad idea and that she's still got a boyfriend no matter how unhappy she is.

There is no big hair or perfect teeth in this scene. We cut rather awkwardly to some time after, when Yon drives Clara, me, and an uncomfortable silence, home to bed.

It is not a very fluid or sensual scene. No awards will be won, no accolades given and none looked for. But it is a scene that makes me feel pretty good about myself, albeit in a selfish, overtly masculine way. It has been a long time since I had this kind of attention, and even though there's a great potential for this situation to blow up in my face, there's something devilishly attractive about it too...

The next day is a celebration of the hangover. Bad things always happen when you don't get one out of the way before manufacturing another. It all equates to bad mathematics: $H + H = H^2$.

But a cure is at hand. Clara and I do the only three things that can possibly deliver us salvation: smoke a joint, eat lots, and do nothing for the rest of the day. Until Yon turns up at the house under some pretext or other, and invites us to go for a ride on the cable car, up the mountain which looks over Caracas. Clara declines but somehow I'm drawn to the occasion, something inside me really wants to go with her, something inside me is quite surprisingly keen in fact. I can't imagine what it is.

Soon the two of us are sitting in a darkened teleférico swinging silently skywards in an expectant and not uncomfortable silence. Cleverly I smuggled a joint with me for exactly this moment. I spark it and the little cabin soon starts to fill with sweet smoke.

'Sorry about last night,' says Yon, taking the offered joint, her face illuminated for a second in orange light as she takes a drag.

'That's okay,' I say, watching the dark trees swing by below us, 'it was just weird, y'know, after spending the day in a cosy little bubble with Maiko.'

'Yeah,' she says on the in breath, passing the joint back to me. 'I just couldn't help it. I was so drunk.'

'Don't worry about it,' I say, trying to make out her face in the dark. We're quiet, and then:

'He treats me like shit you know Wil.' A statement, not a question. I keep my mouth shut. There is silence. Below us the city lights get smaller and smaller, the orderly lines of the main city are mocked by the haphazard, twinkling mayhem of the barrios.

'I like you, you know Wil?' Shifting closer so our bums touch on the seat.

I gulp. *You can't be surprised by this or feign some kind of weak, moral indignation, Wil,* I think to myself. *You knew this was going to happen and that's why you came. You could have stayed at home and read your book like a good boy, but instead you're dangling in the dark with someone else's sexy girlfriend and you're trying to appease your conscience by pretending you didn't know exactly what was going on. Bollocks my friend. It's a 50:50 choice now and you've got to choose.*

Uncle Willy has already chosen.

'Will you stay with me tonight?' She says, looking up at me.

Fuck it.

And I kiss her.

Now it's hard for me to know how far to take this scene. I've probably gone too far already. Shall I carry on and describe in detail the amorous, adulterous fumblings and rockings of a steamy cable car? Or shall I draw a tasteful curtain over the world and fade once again to black? Neither. I shall draw a distracting picture of a kitten. There is something wrong with its legs.

And so I kiss her. And take her pants off. And the pair of us look sheepish and pleased with ourselves when the cable car opens at the top of the mountain and the spotty youth helps us out amid a cloud of weed smoke and musty sex smells. Then we wander about and look down at the city lights for a full five minutes, get bored and make out on the way down the mountain too.

The Toucan, like El Mani, is timeless. The décor hasn't changed since the late fifties. A brass bell on the wattled bar summons a waiter in a yellow tux which matches the furniture, like a colour coordinated genie in a wicker bottle.

We order G and Ts and sit by the pool on ancient loungers and marvel at the place. On the register are Mr and Mrs Lee, and we are timeless too. This place may not even exist. We may not ever leave. Such are the topics of our conversations.

Then we go to bed.

I wake up feeling like a new man. I stretch and yawn and the pornography of the night before slips lazily through my mind. I don't know where Yon is though. I check quickly that she hasn't left. Her panties are on the radiator, trousers by the door. Toilet door closed. Muffled conversation. She's on the phone. I don't care. I'm a man again. I roll over, happily naked, and spark a ciggie.

Then, like all good things, my dreamy morning in bed is brought to an end. She's crying. *Bollocks*. Of course she's crying. She's sitting in the bathroom naked, reeking of infidelity and guilt, talking to her boyfriend on the phone as I lie back puffing away like Humphrey bloody Bogart post coitus. It won't do. So up I get and tidy the room and give her an understanding hug when she limps out of the bathroom sniffing and dribbling.

The car journey back is subdued to say the least. What else could it be?

When I get home Clara is not happy with me. The first waves of guilt start washing over me. What felt at first like a good idea in a cable car half way up a mountain now feels a bit fucking stupid. Fredo has been calling Clara. Clara has been lying for me. Maiko has been calling Clara. Clara has been lying for me.

I hang my head. I can see the proverbial broken windows of Fredo's greenhouse looming jagged on the horizon and I don't like them. People in other people's girlfriends should not throw stones.

So I placate the Claret, tell her all about it and she understands and it's not really me she's angry with but Yon and Fredo and their bullshit, but I should not have gotten involved and it would be wise to skip town for a couple of days. I could not agree more. The perfect opportunity for escape presents itself presently. Little Maiko calls. She's lonely, missing me and driving east with her cousin's friends for a few days. I am invited.

Within a few hours I'm in Maiko's geeky cousin's car, snuggled up on the back seat. For the first, but by no means the last time, I wonder whether it's a good idea to go get stuck for three days with people I don't know, people I might not want to know. These guys are rich. Rich and geeky.

The youngest of Maiko's cousins has one of those voices that sounds like his balls have been meaning to drop for years but never quite made it. The other, his older brother, has private school etched so deeply into him that a bulldozer couldn't budge it.

As we drive out of Caracas, past acres and acres of hillside slums, I realise quickly from their conversations that their view of the world is quite different from mine: they hate Chavez. They hate him with bilious, rabid vindictiveness, with bullet points and diagrams and headings and subheadings and postscripts. It's going to be a long three days. I snuggle closer to Maiko and block out the droning brothers Grimm with a pillow.

You're just tired and short tempered, I tell myself, *you'll be okay in the morning.*

And I slip my hand down the back of Maiko's pants to make myself feel better. She smacks it away and I doze off, wondering for the second, but by no means the last, time why I'm there.

We head east, past Puerto La Cruz, past the beach where I met a family in another lifetime, past the foot of Araguita's valley, past the bus stop where Delores and I said goodbye to Carlos and BB, past it all and on to Cumana.

We eat sensibly, swim sensibly, drink sensibly and avoid the topic of politics sensibly. We are all very sensible. Boring, some might say, but it's better to be safe than sorry, better to be sensible and safe and predictable and dying of boredom than sorry.

I escape now and then for the good of all. I find an unsensible bar and chat to unpredictable old men, I find a posh kid poker game going on by the pool and offer to deal a few hands and leave them sorry with a safe wad of trust fund Bolívares. Full house, jacks over fours. I can't help feeling sorry for them all, the poor loves.

That night Maiko and I sleep together, quietly, clumsily, like kids popping cherries, and wake up shy and smiling sheepishly in the morning.

I spend my last day in Venezuela driving back to Caracas, my tired and bitten tongue rammed against my clenched teeth for fear of giving the cousins a righteous political diatribe. I say a sincerely sad goodbye to Maiko, thank them all for their company and tolerance and rush, as fast as my legs and the soft rock bus can carry me, back to Alto Prado and my Claret.

For a full half hour I squeeze my swollen spleen out to her, my outrage... my pent up fucking outrage at the gall of these blinkered, right-wing types... splutter... wheeze... it's... it's... outrageous! And then I feel much better.

We esmoke a last joint together in the dog piss yard and reminisce about our month together. I was only going to stay for a couple of nights. I love my Claret. Then, as if I haven't had enough already, I call Yon and tell her I have a couple of hours before my flight and ask her if she'd like to take me out for lunch. She isn't happy with me. I ran away and left her up to her knees in emotional garbage. But I am sorry, quite sincerely sorry.

I hug Clara and her dad and wave a tearful goodbye from Yon's car as she turns into the traffic. I am on the road again. My life is in a backpack and I'm almost alone. I look over at Yon and she smiles at me and I smile back at her, very sincerely.

We eat roast chicken and avocado salad and I tell her, without lying once, about what Clara described as 'Asian Success Week'. I tell her how I made a choice between her and Maiko and perhaps I'd made the wrong choice. I tell her about my hatred of love triangles and my apparent inability to stay out of this one. We laugh. We are adults. Life is simple when you're honest.

I lean back in my chair and pick my teeth with a cocktail stick and sigh contentedly.

'You know one thing I regret though, Wil?' says she.

'What's that, Yon?'

'I regret not having slept with you before you left.'

'Blimey.' I say.

In perfect synchronicity we both look at our watches, work out how long I've got till my flight leaves and wave to the waiter. Quietly, efficiently, we pay, leave, get in the car and drive around the corner to Aladdin's Palace; a theme park designed with just this kind of eventuality in mind. A hotel with prices by the hour, parking in the basement, themed rooms, mirrors on the ceilings and understanding, unassuming staff. It's like an X-rated Mr Ben. We have half an hour. No time for the family-size Jacuzzi. I just wish I hadn't eaten so much roast chicken and avocado salad.

Two hours later I'm waiting for a plane bound for Lima, Peru, feeling a bit sticky but rather pleased with myself. Yon and I said our goodbyes in honest-to-god adult fashion and kissed a friendly farewell at the airport bar, just leaving enough time for one last beer.

After check-in and customs I drink another beer and settle in to that almost dangerous feeling of weightlessness I always get when I drink in airports. I am alone. I am free. I survived Venezuela and I am bound far away.

In the bathroom I ask a wizened little janitor where the smoking room is.

'*No hay area de fumar, Señor.*' There isn't one. But, winking, he ushers me into a cubicle and mops a lookout while I smoke my last Belmont, exhaling into the dusty air-con vent. I press my last greasy two thousand Bs note into his hand as I leave.

He calls after me '*Gracias joven. Bon viaje.*'

Part Two

12: Lima

In Lima. Got the squits. Hosbitaje el Dorado. Barranco 54.
LIma. Peru. Where are you? Linden

– was all Linden Dewey wrote. I'd stopped to e-mail Mum
before boarding at Caracas International, having neglected her
for weeks, and in my overflowing inbox, between a band
newsletter I didn't want and an exciting special offer for Viagra,
was Linden's message. He does turn up in the oddest places.

We almost grew up together, Linden and I. In festivals and
parties, when our parents were off with the fairies or the
yogis, we'd run around with the other kids in feral packs
getting into trouble; baggy, hippy-kids with undercuts and
sleeping bags over our skinny shoulders, hanging off the back
of trucks or smoking badly made joints in leaky tents, too
young for that sort of thing and yet somehow older than our
age suggested because of it.

He introduced me to 2000AD and the Freak Brothers,
taught me my first chords and gave me my first mushrooms.
Years later, after being out of touch for seven or eight years,

we met again in a French Connection casting on the Tottenham Court Road. A while after that we lived in a flat in Brixton for a year, playing foosball and reading Robert Crumb comics. A gifted, lanky strider of a man, one of the most naturally bohemian people I know, with a habit of making insane, dangerous friends.

In Lima. Got the squits.

This is going to be different.

It is already different. Lima, Peru. In a greasy, soft-focus haze of pollution and Pacific spray it squats. A squalid tribute to imperialism and dust. Perched above the garbage-sown sand and booming waves of the Pacific, it whines, rumbles and steams.

The airport is like I'd imagined Caracas was going to be: hectic. The people seem to have been shrunk to make room for more of them. Everywhere they scuttle, antlike in energy, childlike in stature, dark brown in colour and hawk-faced.

I'd harboured secret fears about turning up here, though I'm the brown, streetwise traveller again, I was still worried about getting into South America proper. But I see immediately that those fears were groundless. This is definitely a poorer country, the airport itself is largely wooden and antiquated; handrails and banisters have that sweat-greased sheen of age about them, concrete and old tiles crumble everywhere, uniforms are more outdated, the seventies seem to linger in nicotine stains and slacks. But, unlike the M16, jungle-cammo, hip-hop swagger of Venezuela there is no intimidation in this old-world mayhem. I realise straight away that this is the territory of the wheedling hustler, not the tooled up kidnapper.

Bolstered by the knowledge that I'm in a more malleable, less immediate form of danger, I walk out into the warm night.

Outside it's like a twisted Beatles homecoming where screaming, adolescent girls have been replaced by cab drivers and hotel touts. We, the gringos, are the Awesome Foursome. I am Lennon. I refuse to be McCartney.

McCartneys are being ripped-off wholesale, they're positively queuing up to be fleeced. I sit in a proverbial lotus position on my rucksack and smoke a ciggie. I am comfortable, I really am, I am the egg man.

Then I get up, ask a copper politely, conspiratorially how much a cab to Barranco should cost and then beat down a cabbie with a practised squint, a spit and a judicious raise of the eyebrows.

With chaotic energy, life flows past the windows of my cab. Markets and pedestrian streets roar with an endless flood of people, small, dark, weathered people.

Policemen and soldiers are everywhere, as if a revolution might break out at any time. Old yellow Bluebird school buses from the States have been re-invented as troop transporters, spray-painted khaki green, the old familiar 'school bus' letters still showing through under the new 'Policía' stencils, daubed in dribbling, white letters.

Where once dangled the happy little legs of American school-children now dangle the angry, scared little legs of Peruvian riot police. Where once sat a town of Amerindian fishermen and farmers now hunkers a vast and haphazard metropolis.

As we cruise through the hazy streets and down onto the coast road which skirts the booming Pacific I ask the driver what's going on in Lima, what the police are like and how the politicians are, how the people are feeling. In Venezuela these questions were invariably answered with enthusiastic and heartfelt openness, an eagerness to share information and to tell it like it is. The Peruvians are different, starting from now: Ready? Steady? Shut up.

Lima according to the cabbie: The police are friendly, fair and uncorrupt. The politicians are likewise and the people are very happy, thank you very much for asking.

We slow to a stop at a set of traffic lights and a train of shopping trolleys trundles by, full of rubbish, plastic bottles and cardboard. The ragged cowpokes on this rattling roundup look up briefly with hungry, tired eyes. Then they shuffle off into the night.

'I see what you mean,' I tell the cabbie sarcastically, 'these people look like they're having a great time.'

In Barranco the cabbie insists that we'd haggled the fare in Yankee dollars not Peruano soles. I stare at him for a few seconds, trying to read an emotion behind his black pearl eyes. I cannot. Neither can I be bothered to argue. This man is not going to budge, so I pay up. Welcome to Peru, little white man, welcome to Peru.

Welcome to Barranco. Welcome to an old semi-detached townhouse converted into dorm rooms, chillout rooms, TV rooms and shared kitchens. Welcome to a hostel for the first time in a month and a half.

Welcome to padlocks on the fridge and hand-drawn posters advertising cut price tours and Extreme! expeditions. Welcome to house rules and name-tagged supernoodle cupboards. Welcome to handsome Linden Dewey already telling the young American guy behind the reception desk to skin up for him, already demanding this and that from the gaggle of already devoted disciples surrounding him.

Welcome to a beer and a spliff and a dawning realisation that life has just changed dramatically again: I am no longer a member of the Caracas arty party scene. I am no longer a novelty. I am no longer part of a culture. I am a backpacker, like the rest of these floppy-haired, gap-year, trust-fund, temporary runaways. I am the froth on the surface of life. I am White Man.

Peru, with its Machu Picchus and Nazcar lines, has drawn tourists like us for generations. For so many generations, in fact, that some Peruvians have evolved to become experts in the subtle arts of tourist deception and hustling. But who can blame them? If I was born into a poor family, in a poor country, on a poor continent I too would probably be a hustler. I don't begrudge them their hustle, only my place in it.

I am astounded by the number of tourists here. It's hard to believe that there are any rosy-cheeked, well-fed, well-schooled English kids left in England. Don't get me wrong, I don't hate them, only their place in this hustle.

Already I've heard too many conversations about which countries and sights these kids have 'done', where they're going to 'do' next and where isn't worth 'doing' at all. I pity them for all their 'doing' because while they're 'doing' what they're 'doing' they're really getting 'done'.

But who am I to talk like that? I'm as bad as any of them, perhaps worse, because I grew up in a place that was regularly 'done' by tourists and I know how it feels. So I try hard not to 'do' places. I try, for the short time that I'm in a place, just to 'be' there, to see how it would be without me, to see how it really works, its truth. But, however I paint it, it all equates to the same thing: I come, I spend a little money, I steal a little of a place's soul and then I leave. And when I'm gone the place where I've been feels cheated and abused because I can come and go as I please and it cannot, its people, they cannot. You can't enter an environment without altering it, and likewise you can't leave without taking something with you, without leaving something behind.

But it's good to see old Dewey again and, in a sense, it's good to have an appreciative audience of young greenhorns to make us feel like old campaigners. So we drink beer and I tell stories of Caracas and Venezuela, gorged with exaggeration. The same romantic horror stories people told me before I went there.

'It's a war out there kids, I'm lucky to have made it here at all.'

Then I drift off to sleep in my bunk, soothed by the snoring around me and the smell of feet. Not very long ago I was in Aladdin's Palace, watching Yon's lovely round behind in a round mirror above a round bed. Now I'm bedding down with the forty chiefs.

Who'd have thought, eh? Who'd have thought...

13: La Merced and Talmar

On the night Linden and I leave town a girl called Mandy Stowe enters it. I'm packing and drinking beer in the hostel reception when she walks in from the Amazon: a mixed-race Manchester lass with coffee skin and a wayward afro. It isn't a Maiko Mao moment but our eyes do meet, something does draw us together.

'Alright?' I say, looking up from my rucksack, a pair of socks in my hand.

'Yeah,' she says, turning round to look at me.

'Where you been?' I ask, stuffing the socks down into my pack.

'Up in the jungle,' she says in a heavy Mancunian accent.

'What was it like?' I ask.

'Hot,' she says, 'and full of bloody mozzies.'

We sit down and drink a beer together. I like her, she's cute but not girly, proud and feisty. She laughs at me and gives me a few Valium for our bus ride. There's no romance in our exchange, more a flirtatious sparring, checking each other out.

Then we leave, Linden, me, our worldly possessions in two small backpacks, Linden's guitar, some Valium, a bag of weed and two bus tickets to the most remote place accessible in a night's travel. A place described by my guide book as 'uninteresting'. We leave, and immediately our bunks and roles are filled by another two just like us, for we are many, we privileged few.

I sit back in my comfortable seat and read half a page of my book. Then the Valium kicks in and immediately I'm asleep. In my dreams I'm on a bus hurtling down narrow roads on impossibly steep hills. There's no structure to the dreams, no storyline, just hills and speed and squealing brakes.

When I wake up daylight is streaming in through cracks in the curtains. Linden is awake beside me, his eyes wide and excited. He describes the country we've been travelling through and wonders at my ability to sleep through lurching downhill slaloms and screaming brake pads. In the night we crossed the Andes and now we're heading towards the suburbs of the Amazon.

La Merced is just such a suburb, crouching among the forested foothills of the Andes beside a roaring river of clay-brown water. The air is fresh and wet, cool in the morning mist, heavy with the mossy scent of trees and earth.

There is no crowd to meet us, no hustlers or touts, just an old lady selling roasted corn and bottled water. With the Valium still working its way though me I'm peaceful; everything is drowsy and dreamlike. Smiling we wander up the muddy road towards town. It's like a scene from a Mervyn Peake story: an expanse of mildewed masonry and rusted corrugated iron perched on the sodden hillside, its buildings set in blocks like Manhattan, though any similarity ends there. La Merced is a trading town, an outpost, a last gasp of civilisation before the Amazon begins, and when it begins it doesn't end for hundreds of miles.

The shops lining the grubby main street sell machetes and

cowboy hats, greased tools and sacks of wheat and corn, green coffee beans and little orange and yellow potatoes.

We find a café on the roadside, just a small room open to the street on two sides where a few locals sit on stools, eating fried egg sandwiches and drinking coffee.

We pile our bags against the wall and order the same, watched with amusement by the other customers.

It is clear from the interested, humorous looks of passers-by that we have left the Tourist Saturation Zone, the Gringo Resentment Field, the Hustlers Quadrant of Fleecing and Dollar Relievement, and we are relieved.

We sit back contentedly and watch the early-morning traffic on the road: a shabby parade of motor rickshaws, cattle, trucks, mules and taxis. The fried egg sandwiches are good and the people are friendly, and in this harmonious atmosphere of full stomachs and tranquillity we wander further up the hill to find a hostel.

We travel well together, Linden and I, there is so much history between us that we immediately settle in our time-honoured roles as friends. We find a hostel just as it starts to rain and sit on our wool-blanketed beds and smoke a few spliffs, watching the rain drip from the wooden eaves outside the window and the rusted roofs beyond, conscious of how far the sound of our laughter and guitar playing is travelling and what it must sound like in the misty streets.

We have decided that learning a few songs on the guitar, to perform in times of need, is the right thing to do. A couple of Johnny Cash numbers, Neil Diamond's 'Solitary Man' and an old country tune my folks sing, the chorus of which goes like this:

Please don't bury me
down in the cold, cold ground.

I'd rather have them cut me up
and pass me all around.
You can throw my brain to the hurricane
and the blind can have my eyes.
The deaf can take both my ears
if they don't mind the size.

It feels good to sit and sing, to laugh at subtle, old jokes, to be in such an odd and foreign place and yet feel so at home.

Later we sit in the little square in the middle of town and drink a few beers. Peru are playing Ecuador tonight in a world cup qualifier and a huge screen has been erected at the far end of a little park. It is still raining.

I sit on a bench and strum quietly while Linden makes friends with the local winos. An old, toothless man is trying to set him up with a slightly younger toothless woman. I don't share Linden's love of bums. I have nothing particularly against them. I just don't need friends like these; dangerous, smelly friends.

Linden does. He loves them and shows his love by borrowing my money to buy more beer for the bums. Soon he is king of the bums and I am his sodden, surly sidekick. Soon we are drunken singing bums ourselves, singing drunkenly at the rain, strumming to the misty jungle hills, howling like horny cats and gnashing our teeth at passers by. This is how I immerse myself in foreign cultures: I get down and dirty with its winos and sing to its rains.

That night we sit among the steaming populace in the square and watch the football. Throughout the match we try to instil in them a British appreciation of the game, but to no avail. They are just too naturally docile, too quiet for songs like 'You're going home in a fucking ambulance' and 'You couldn't score in a brothel'.

Linden is hounded incessantly by his wino subjects, they shuffle around him demanding more beer and ciggies, while I, in my capacity as 'the unfriendly one', watch with delight the fruits of Linden's misdirected labour.

When his bummy admirers become too insistent we stagger away from the crowd to find a party, any party, there must be a party. After a while, walking down a dead-end street, we stumble across the inviting sound of pool balls clicking and glasses clinking. Behind a huge iron door we find an ornate and ancient pool hall. Long, dark and smoky, its high ceilings are a brown mess of cobwebs and moulded plaster. The only light comes from the bare bulbs hung on long wires above the tables.

Instinctively we order more beer and pool cues, and sit back on wooden stools to watch an argument between a group of young Peruanos and the balding patron. We are amused, we two, made naturally fearless by the fact that we're so much bigger than these little men. Naturally aware that we would have at least a stone and a foot over anyone in the room. That's how my brain works anyway; Linden is a little different. Linden likes to find the most dangerous people he can and make friends with them. Soon the swaying pair of us are sharing beers with the agitators, soon we have a bunch of new dangerous friends.

They are from the city, I don't remember which, in La Merced on business, I don't remember what. I don't like them immediately. I am drunk and sick of drunks, restless and horny and sullen. Linden is jovial, energetic and friendly. We play a classic good-cop/bad-cop routine: Linden lulls them into a false sense of security and I behave just erratically enough to make them feel uncomfortable. Out of boredom rather than hostility we play our parts, hustling doubles games for beers, swaggering and tough in our six feet of bone and twelve stone of flesh. But none of it matters, eleven stone five feet of water and the rest a sticky mass of calcium, carbon and bullshit.

In my memory the night ends in a fuzz of white noise and alcohol-induced brain damage. According to Linden I was rude to our new friends. According to Linden they invited us to stay in their house, but one of them kept touching my arm and chest as he spoke so I told him to get the fuck away from me and invited his friends outside, if they cared to come. According to Linden I went home soon after they declined my offer. I think Linden thinks I may be a little mad. Maybe I am. Or maybe I just don't like strange dudes touching me.

The days that follow see us on much the same mission of excess. We drink one morning on the banks of the fast, dirty river after buying Stetsons and button-down, short-sleeved shirts. We strip down to our underwear, wade out into the thigh-deep water and cling to rocks, our bodies skipping on the surface of the current. Then we sit on our haunches and drip dry, drink our beer, slap at huge black mosquitoes and sing our songs. Thus the days slip grubbily by until we can take no more, and with no planned destination we head back to the bus station and take the next bus out of town.

It happens to be going west, into the mountains, up to a dusty little town called Talmar, high in the Andes. Upwards the roads climb, and as they do the air gets thinner, the chasms below us become deeper, and the land more barren. To boys who grew up in Welsh hill-country these towering mountains, which in truth are only foothills by Andean standards, are outrageous in their scale, the valleys our little bus bumbles through are so high that the ridges seem almost to meet above us.

Our guide book, happily enough, has very little to say for Talmar, apart from its proximity to the longest cave system on the continent and a dilapidated yet 'interesting' Inca ruin. It has little else of worth to 'do', and that suits us just fine.

Talmar, like La Merced, is a town dwarfed by its environment, a town cowed by its surrounding landscape. Talmar saw La Merced's Amazon suburb and raised it an Andes. La Merced folded. If any one word could be used to describe Talmar it would be 'dusty'. 'Dry' or 'desolate' don't quite cut it, being words dependent on perspective. 'Drab' or 'monotonous' aren't far off the mark but they don't fill your throat and eyes with soil or your clothes with filth. It is a town built almost entirely of large clay bricks, a town surrounded by dusty, high-altitude fields. Any town built out of dust, dependent on dust, is bound to be dusty.

When the bus stops we clamber wearily down and stretch our crushed limbs. The bus was so small, the roads so bad and our fellow passengers so smelly that the journey became an interesting new endurance test rather than a jolly sightseeing tour. After a brief and uninspired inspection of Talmar we hole up in an ancient, empty hostel built in colonial style with a covered courtyard in the middle. The rooms are high ceilinged and comfy and the wooden floors creak so loud we have to walk pressed against the wall so as not to wake each other up at night.

We ran out of weed a few days ago and have been drinking so much that our bodies need a rest. So that evening, after exhausting our patience for card games and books, we wander out, looking for some action.

Along the four or five blocks of well lit streets, Linden and I now walk, in search of youths or undesirable characters who'll lead us to a smoke. We don't have to wait long. As we wander down the main street the quintessential undesirable character wobbles up to us on an old bicycle. He's almost Dickensian, dressed in fingerless gloves and a long coat, a slippery character from a mile off, worse when you can smell him.

There are two types of undesirables in towns small and

large around the world. The first is truly undesirable. He will go out of his way to lie to you, steal from you and cheat you as much as you allow him to. He is the unscrupulous bastard who sold me a bag of oregano in Camden market when I was a teenager, the same shady figure who ripped me off in India on my first week there, the very same miserable burden who has robbed me so many times in different guises that I now recognise him immediately.

The second type of undesirable is slightly more desirable than the first. While regarded by society as a dangerous vagabond he is often, in fact, a perfectly legitimate business-man with kids to feed and quotas to meet. He'll want simply to sell you what he can and make a profit. He will, like any successful businessman, be happiest with a regular client base of people he knows, therefore he will not try to rip you off. Opportunism is the name of Type Number One's game, consistency the priority for Type Number Two.

The ragged cyclist we see before us is a Type Number One through and through. Predictably Linden thinks otherwise, and while I slip casually into bad cop and politely seek to get rid of him Linden borrows some more money off me, makes a deal for a bag of weed, money up front, to be delivered to the main plaza in half an hour.

'The trouble with you, Wil, is that you don't trust people enough.'

'Hmmm,' says me, with a sardonic raise of the left eyebrow. 'We'll see.'

We saw. Linden waited for an hour out in the cold while I snuggled up in bed and read my book.

'The trouble with you,' I say, when he creaks back to the room empty handed, 'is that you trust people too much.'

The next night we try again. This time we work on the Bi-Typical Dealer system. This time I am in charge.

Down by the cake shop, on a paved section of street, a group of lads are hanging out. It seems that youth culture worldwide is united these days. Even in remote Peruvian mountain towns the kids look little different to those in towns anywhere. I suppose satellite TV and the internet are mainly responsible for this unity. The group of youths hanging out in dusty old Talmar are wearing Korn and Slipknot T-shirts, hoodies and baseball caps. Listening to 50 Cent and J-Lo. Their parents' generation must have looked a lot like the generations before them: sensible and practical in their bright shawls, ponchos and rigid hats. Now, thanks to MTV and a massive trade in fake designer clothes, the current generation can look as much like suburban American teens as they want and still know nothing about the people they are emulating, or the world in which they exist.

Sickening though this plague of consumerism may be, it does make buying weed off punk kids in foreign cultures a lot easier. Just find the dopey-looking one in the Bob Marley T-shirt and make friends with him. There he is, just over there, hanging out with his friends outside the cake shop, drinking Pisco.

We hang back for a bit and suss them out: there are about seven of them, all in their late teens, they look harmless enough. So we wander over and ask, in bad Spanish, if they know where we could get a smoke. They are delighted. Of course they know where to get weed, come and sit down, have a drink and I'll go off and get some for you.

Now, Bob Marley boy looks like a Type Two, but you can never be too careful. So we decide that Linden should go with him and I should stay and hang out with his mates.

This is how I immerse myself in foreign cultures: I buy a group of teenagers a bottle of sweet grape liquor and proceed to do shots with them until we're all thoroughly wasted.

In about an hour Linden returns with Bob Marley, a wee bag of green, a happy smile and pink eyes. We spend the rest of the night hanging out with the lads: a cultural exchange session of rum, Tekken, foosball and weed in various seedy establishments around town. Culminating in an odd little jam session on the dusty floor of an abandoned house, candles and bottles and long shadows on the wall.

The next day Linden and I decide that we need a little more action. There is only so much 'being' a man can put up with before he needs to 'do' something. And so, with that in mind, we pack camping and cooking equipment for the night, buy multi-coloured soup, veg and coca leaves from the little old Cholas in the market and a blanket from a little old Cholo in a smelly blanket shop. Then we blag a lift in a little old VW towards the next village, the village with the caves.

The valleys we now pass through, though shallower than the ones we passed through before, are no less impressive. The rocky cliffs are draped with hanging moss which the driver calls 'Jesus' beard' and the fields of the valley floor, next to the stream, explode with flowers, red and yellow tulips, purple irises, pink mallows and little blue forget-me-not.

The village is even smaller and dustier than Talmar. It has no paved road, just a dried-up, cracked fountain in a dusty plaza, a dusty store and a dusty little café.

We find the route out of town painted in dribbling, red letters on a mud wall. An arrow points us up and out of the village though a small valley beside a bright little trout stream, past gardens and pigs and llamas and shy little locals in shawls and bowler hats.

We stuff coca leaves into our cheeks the way an old man showed us, and trudge up the shabby path, now and then spitting out great plumes of green juice in fine wild-west fashion. A little way up the track we meet the first gringos we've seen in this high country.

'Hello,' we say.

'Hello,' they say back.

'How's the cave?' we ask.

'It's good,' they answer.

Then there's nothing else to say, so we say goodbye. Then we walk away quietly, the sense of isolation and wildness knocked out of us. They were a funny looking bunch, those gringos, though I guess they could say the same thing about us, in our Stetsons and shirts.

The cave is funny looking too: out of a hole in the barren mountainside gushes a clear stream on whose mossy banks has been planted a rather kitsch garden of topiary and rhododendrons. An equally kitsch little picnic area has been erected on the flat land of the valley floor. In the centre of all that is dusty, high-altitude and remote stands an ice cream hut, a lawn decorated lovingly with covered picnic tables and flower borders and a lad with a roll of tickets and a money belt. Our sense of adventure wilts. But what can you do? There's no wood for a fire, no space to camp among the rocks and bogs of the valley floor, none better than the lawn and anyway it's starting to get dark. So, resigned to our rather kitsch fate, we buy tickets from the wee ticket man, open a beer and get out the guitar. As soon as we sit down three snotty little kids materialise and immediately begin climbing all over us and our packs, giggling incessantly and stinking of sour milk and poo. Like a lot of kids I've seen at high altitude their cheeks are a purplish red mess of burst capillaries and their lips are cracked and sore-looking.

I like kids. Kids like me. It's a mutual understanding and I like it that way. At first I like these kids. At first they like me. But this mutual understanding doesn't last long. At first we give them apples and carrots which they devour ravenously, Linden let's them help him play guitar and they decide to help me put up the tent. At this point our mutual affection begins to wane. The more I ask them not to walk on the tent, the more they giggle and do just that. Then we buy a bag of nearly green eucalyptus logs for an embarrassingly extortionate price from a little house upstream and set about making a fire and chopping veg. Then it starts to rain. The kids poke at the damp, pathetic fire and it goes out. They walk mud onto the food and giggle constantly. I am growing furious.

I like kids. Kids like me. I like being outdoors, camping and cooking my own food on an open fire. It's my thing. But not today. Today my fire is shit. Today it is raining. Today we're camping in a quaint little picnic area in the middle of the wild Andes. Today I don't need little snotnoses giving me a hard time. Feeling like a tyrant, I yell at them and send them away. Linden looks at me like I'm a maniac. I hang my head. Our soup won't boil. We scour the fields and the riverbank for wood but find only a pitiful, soggy amount. Then it starts to rain even harder.

At high altitude the boiling point of water gets lower. This means that our yellow spuds and veg take much longer to cook, this means that we sit for much longer than expected next to our hissy little fire in the rain, this means that we are not very happy, not very happy chappies at all. Eventually, with the sack that once carried the wet wood over our wet shoulders, we eat our soup semi-raw. It's tasty enough, but a little crunchier than I like it.

Unwilling to sit miserably in the tent for the rest of the evening and even less willing to sit outdoors we take the guitar and remaining bottles of beer and dry ciggies up to the cave. The main entrance is a little further up than the stream outlet, it yawns above us in the dark, stalactites hanging from its roof like twisted fangs, huge and gaping. A little forbidding and overly dramatic for this time of night, but at least it's dry.

We walk a little way in, find a corner out of the wind, light a candle and open our beers. There we sit for the rest of the evening, our bums turning numb on the damp cave floor, our breath steaming and billowing around us, our shadows thirty feet high on the cave wall, flickering and dancing, a cowboy hat, a guitar and an occasional ten foot beer bottle in wriggling silhouette. And we sing:

> *...don't know if I will*
> *but until I can find me*
> *a girl who'll stay*
> *and won't play games behind me*
> *I'll be what I am*
> *A solitary man...*

That night I dream about Mandy Stowe, the mixed-race girl who gave us the Valium in Lima. It isn't a particularly memorable dream, just a feeling of warmth and companionship: a happy, smiley dream that leaves me feeling lonely afterwards.

The next morning I am woken up, bright and early, by a kick in the head. I'd be alarmed, even frightened, if a constant, high-pitched giggle didn't accompany the kick. I wake Linden up, running viciously through my limited Spanish swearword repertoire and fumbling desperately with the zip. He looks at me like I'm a maniac again, but this time I don't feel guilt, this time I feel rage, good British disgust for Johnny Foreigner and a ferocious need to bury my foot in something smelly and giggling. Then I give up and go back to sleep.

The day after that Linden's granddad dies. We're in an internet café back in Talmar when he finds out. We'd made it back easily enough, feeling a bit saggy after our disappointing adventure. (Though I did eat guinea pig for the first time – the only meal on the menu of the dusty little village café. At least I think it was guinea pig.)

Linden looks pretty shaken by the news. He had been close to his granddad. So in good Celtic fashion we decide that we should hit the bottle then and there and not stop till the old man's been given a decent send off. It's eleven in the morning.

Now it just so happens that a couple of days ago Linden met a guy from Lima called Raphael. Raphael is living in Talmar doing some unspecified variety of work. He's a pretty seedy looking dude, but he gave Linden some weed when they first met so we like him. On the way to get drunk we meet Raphael outside a café. We tell him about our mission and he decides to join our noble cause.

We start with cake and coffee from the cake shop to line our stomachs, keeping an eye out through the plate glass window for the Dickensian Type Number One with the bike. Then we move on to the rum. Raphael suggests that street-drinking might be frowned upon by the pious people of Talmar so perhaps we should drink in his house.

We follow him through a maze of crumbling streets, far from the paved and uppity town centre, bottles clinking in plastic bags. Up a rotten flight of stairs we follow him, past doors hiding screaming kids and sour cooking smells, past doors hiding weed smoke, past holes in the floor and rats in the ceiling, out onto a parapet and into another building and eventually to the cracked wooden door of his apartment.

The floor and walls are bare except for a few magazine pages taped above the bed. We're ushered in and told to sit on the rickety, unmade bed and roll a spliff from the pile of weed he presents us. Then he scuttles out and comes back with four plastic cups and a bespectacled neighbour. The neighbour is a painter and a man of great wisdom. I recognise this by the way he quietly sits down and pours us all huge, straight rums in plastic cups and raises a toast to Linden's gramps.

'To the grandfather of Linden,' he says in clumsy English.

We drink. Then we smoke. Then we drink some more. The morning sun shines wanly through the dirty window, the sounds of the lives around us filter through the cracked walls and the weed smoke hangs in lazy spirals in the air.

'To the old man,' we say again and drink some more.

This goes on for hours; by dinnertime we are plastered. As usual my memory can't quite cope with the chronology of events that evening. I remember eating chicken and chips somewhere. Raphael is telling us about something, waving his fork around expressively. His hand lingers for a moment under Linden's nose and, for reasons best known to Linden, he leans forward and bites it. Raphael gives a roar of pain which I, in my wasted state, take to be some kind of Peruvian battle cry and promptly put my fork to his throat to keep him in line. There follows a deadlocked few seconds as Raphael looks with big, bloodshot eyes from Linden to me, to the fork and back to Linden. Then we all just seem to forget the whole thing and go on eating and drinking.

The evening ends abruptly a little while later. It is hazy in my mind, but I think Raphael asked me to lend him a hundred bucks. I think I told him to go fuck himself.

On our way to the bus stop, a couple of days later, we meet him coming the other way. He looks like he hasn't stopped drinking since that night. He's wearing the same clothes and his eyes are bloodshot and sullen. He apologises again and again for what he'd said to make me angry. So much so, that I still wonder what really went on.

We leave him and Talmar behind soon after, as stoned as we can get to make the bus journey back to Lima more bearable. As it turns out we needn't have worried, for in the great lottery that is life in Peru we stumble onto one of the five clean, comfortable buses in the country. Our seats recline, our legs have room and the smell of our fellow passengers, although pungent, is not entirely overpowering. So we recline, we stretch out our legs and through the pretty haze of our stoned minds we watch the Andes rumble hugely by.

14: Saigon... Shit... I'm still only in Lima

I wake up in a dorm room bunk with the drums of hell pounding in my head. What was once my mouth is now a sticky, sour gash in the aching sack of my face. I open my ragged eye holes and squint up at the ceiling fan. It rattles and whines, chopping wearily at the stuffy air, assaulting my ears and confusing my eyes. I wince and slowly drop my feet off the bed, then I wait in muted agony as a wave of nausea washes over me. Linden is passed out on a bunk next to me, his eyes half-open, showing only bloodshot whites. He may or may not be breathing.

I lie like that for a while, my feet on the floor, my body on the bed, my bladder as tight as a basketball against my stomach. *I have to piss. Now.* I hesitate, my fractured mind weighs up the consequences of pissing where I lie. Then I push myself off the bed, onto my hands and knees, and crawl towards the door. All around me corpses snore and stink, scum collected in the corners of their gaping maws. It is disgusting. I am disgusting. I try to pull myself up onto my feet but manage only a crouching cower. I grasp the doorknob and fight down another wave of nausea, my mouth fills with saliva and bile.

I slowly swing the door open and the sunlight hits me as if it were made of bricks. I imagine screaming through too-long canines and dead white gums, my skin searing and blistering, my pupils slitted like a cat's. I feel my way down the bright hall in nothing but my underwear, moaning softly to myself, past a chirpy TV room full of happy little backpackers eating lunch. One or two of them say perky hellos but I just growl and bare my teeth at them and scrabble my way towards the toilet, upon whose cool seat I sit like a girl and piss and piss, sighing and moaning still, holding onto the walls as if they might fall away and expose me.

When I'm done I stay sitting there for a very long time, my head in my hands, still moaning. After a while I take an inventory of my mind. I am Wil Gritten. I am in Lima, Peru. It is March or April or something. Last night I...

fuckI'mgoingtobesick... bleaughhh... mmmm... BLEAUGH! ... ooooh... BLEAUGHHHH!... mmmm... ooooh... ohrightup thebackofthenose... bleaugh... thatsbetter... ooooh...

Last night I did some drinking. Linden was there... (belch)... so was Mandy Stowe... I dreamt about her... Oh shit did I kiss her?... Fuckithurtstothink... ooooh.

I make no sense. I sit on the toilet in my underwear with spit hanging from my face and make no sense at all. Why is it so important for me to rack my poor brains when they're at their least responsive? I give up and crawl towards the shower. A sprightly young thing is washing his expensive teeth at the outdoor sink.

'Borning!' he guffaws at me through a mouthful of toothpaste.

'Fuck you,' I reply, as amiably as possible.

'Mumph,' he says and spits indignantly into the sink.

'Wanker,' I mumble to myself and slouch down in the shower, still in my pants. I turn the water on. It's cold, really cold. I scream and thrash about for a bit but then the water starts doings wonderful things to my cerebellum so I sit back, gasp for breath and sizzle. I try the inventory again. I was here for the beginning of the night, drinking Pisco and vodka

Redbulls. Then someone put a mirror and a note in front of me. Mandy was there but we were playing games with each other. I thought it'd be a good idea to treat her like I wanted nothing to do with her... what a dickhead... then we were chatting and happy but still being aloof and semi-detached... then there's a gap... then we're all out at some club and there's some dudes who looked like trouble... then we're sitting with them... then I think Mandy was sitting on my knee and... I was taking the piss out of her picky afro and... oh my head hurts.

I give up again and turn off the water. My underwear is now see-though. I stand there shivering, cupping my tackle with both hands like a little boy, hating myself for getting so wasted, for forgetting important information, and for not bringing a towel with me.

It takes a further three hours for Linden to come back to life. Half an hour after that Mandy appears. I'd spent the hours since I got up eating bacon and eggs and avoiding people, twitching and shaking, sunglasses on constantly against the sun's onslaught.

Mandy and I smile wanly at each other, her inventory more ragged even than mine I guess. Linden whinges and rolls a joint and we smoke it gratefully, flopped on couches and hammocks, forcing back nausea. We communicate in groans and croaks, occasionally laughing and pleading:

'Oh, please don't, it hurts.'

Then Linden gets up to play ping pong and Mandy squeezes in beside me on the couch.

'I don't really remember much about last night,' she says in her thick Manc accent, her brown knees good enough to eat. 'Did we have fun?'

'I don't think so,' I tell her softly, remembering that this is how we speak to each other: intimately taking the piss. 'I think we might have had a bit of a snog.'

'Yeah,' she replies, playing coy, 'I think we might have.'

She smells nice and it feels so comforting to be next to her in my hungover state.

'Wanna get some lunch with me?' I ask, to get her away and have her to myself.

'Alright,' she says and digs me in the ribs.

We sit at a wooden table in an old café full of fading black and white photos and Peruvian businessmen, eating ceviche and drinking soft drinks from glass bottles with straws. It's easy company, we laugh and take the piss out of each other pleasantly.

'You're not bad looking for a daft cow,' I tell her.

'You're not bad yourself, for a fookin Welsh twat,' she says back.

She's a cutie is Mandy Stowe, in her late twenties, white mum, African dad, lovely smile and little freckles on her nose. We seem to have relaxed in each other's company since last night. We'd circled and sized each other up, exchanged insults and taunts which became sweeter and sweeter as the night went on until we were crooning out the cusses, our noses an inch apart, serenading each other with potty-mouth and filth.

We walk down to the beach and fill the holes in each other's memories, holding hands and softly trying to gross each other out. The beach is nasty – trash buried in the sand and lumps of broken masonry everywhere, but we sit down anyway and watch the sunset and the gangs of ragged youths looking for the easy targets.

'I had a dream about you, you know?' I sop.

'You told me last night,' she stiffens.

'I did?' I stiffen too.

'Yeah. You wouldn't shut up about it.' Still stiff.

'Shit... sorry.' Stiffer.

'That's alright, you fookin knob-end.' Less stiff, a smile.

'It was a shit dream anyway. You looked like more of a spaz than you usually do.'

Soppiness averted, stiffness subsides. Soppiness is obviously not cool.

On the stairs which lead back up the cliff to Barranco we kiss again, horny, cursing bunk beds and dorm rooms. Then we walk hand in hand back to the hostel.

Linden is playing ping pong. We buy beers and start the merry-go-round again. Mandy and I settle back into taking the piss and play fighting, occasionally pinning each other against the wall in the corridor or the bathroom for a snog when nobody's looking. Linden says there's a party at the house of some film director he met last night, a pre-wrap, wrap-party for a movie they're shooting in Lima. So we put on clean clothes and troop out into the warm, darkening streets to hail cabs, dodge traffic and watch the night wander by.

It's a good party. Good to be back with the real people of America Latina instead of the visitors. Good to be in a nice apartment drinking wine and meeting old Argentinean actors and Peruvian intellectuals. Good to hear an honest view of the country. Peru according to a Peruvian guy in the film industry: The politicians and the police are horribly corrupt. Foreign multinationals are draining resources. The government is helping them. The people are starving and growing angry. Something will have to give soon. Maybe revolution and guerrilla war. Maybe just more demonstrations and riots. I think about the school bus/police vans, the water cannons and the little men strutting about in military uniforms. I remember the shopping trolley train and the ragged kids on the beach. Then I remember Chavez and Venezuela and I sigh.

Linden is talking about heading north, Lucy's getting in from Colombia tomorrow. She'll probably want to head south and

I feel like I should travel with her for a while. Mandy doesn't know what she's doing but she has to be in Brazil in a couple of months. Maybe she'd like to come south with Lucy and me. Maybe she'd like to sleep in my bed. Maybe at last we can get away from bunk beds and dorm rooms.

Me, I'm just going to go where the wind takes me. In fact I'm going to be the wind, as long as I get to share a room with Mandy and make my peace with Lucy, and as long as I'm in Chile to catch my plane in about four months. Otherwise Latin America is my oyster. I am the wind and America Latina is my oyster.

Chapter 15: Cuzco

In Caracas, Venezuela, a city of fifteen million people, there are no Irish pubs. In the remote little town of Cuzco, Peru, there are two. There are also more white, middle-class people here than there are in the whole of gentrified Brixton and enough novelty ponchos and alpaca socks to keep the whole of Russia warm for decades.

Cuzco is gringo-fever ground zero, hustle HQ, the great Machu Picchu's home town, the quintessence of all that is worth 'doing' in Peru. It is the golden child of glossy tourist brochures, the arsehole of south America out of which the sun is rumoured to shine. It is the nub, the hub and the death place of the legendary John Peel.

Evidence of the sophistication and maturity of Cuzco's hustle is everywhere. Skilled professionals must have been flown in from Morocco, Egypt and India to train the locals in hustling boot-camps. Every gimmick is used with incredible accuracy and skill, every tourist trap polished and oiled, every ingratiating smile shined to perfection. The world and everyone agrees that Machu Picchu is a must-see, the perfect excuse for a Third World spending spree, but it all looks pretty rotten to me. For the bastards have us trapped. The sound of every step on Cuzco's dusty streets, every wheezing breath on its high-altitude stairways, is accompanied by the sound of one hard sell or another.

'Alpaca! Alpaca!' is the cry around the hillsides, and verily it is answered, verily it is bought. Again I must stress that I bear the hustlers no ill will. I am merely pissed at being priced out of the picnic because I don't have the necessary two hundred bucks to see what I'm told I *must* see; the permit to see the ruins costs an arm and a leg, the train up there costs another couple of limbs, and the obligatory guide costs a further few pounds of flesh. In all only my head would be left to roll around the ruins and see what it can. Poor head. So we plot a plan, Mandy, Lucy and I. We decide to arm ourselves with enough marching powder, lightweight gear and SAS spirit to make it up the supposed eighteen clicks of train track to the big M.P. We decide that going at night is the key, as the trains only run during the day and thus we'll be there long before the first gringos get up in the morning. It's a perfect plot, simple and effective, no chance of getting lost, just a nice wee stroll in the hills. Or not. Lucy and I aren't getting on too well. Over the past few weeks, as we travelled through this dusty, high country together, we've grown more and more grumpy. When we met again in Lima she was brown and excited after her time in Colombia and we were old friends again, but as time passed and the towns we passed through became more remote and inhospitable, as I gave up cigarettes because of the altitude and the fact that I was carrying too many bad habits, and as Mandy and I grew closer, tensions started to rise.

We sit in an 'old style' restaurant and eat thin soup and garlic bread and ignore each other. Mandy is trying to keep the party happy. I'm at my worst.

'Listen Wil,' says Lucy after a while, 'if you can't be bothered to walk up there just tell us and we can get moving again.'

'That seems fair, Wil,' says Mandy, fairly.

'Bollocks,' says me through a mouthful of garlic bread. 'This place is shit but we have to go to Machu fucking Picchu because it's why we came all the way to fucking Cuzco. I just hate these little fuckers ripping me off and calling me a cunt all the time. It's fucking bullshit.'

'Okay Wil,' says Lucy, losing patience. 'Why don't you just find out how far it is and get a map or something and work it out from there?'

'Fuck off,' says me.

'That's not fair, Wil,' says Mandy fairly.

'Okay. We'll find a map, but I guarantee you these little cunts have fucked it for us so we can't get up there. They've fucked everything else for us. Fuck, I can't fucking breathe!'

'Jesus!' Lucy yells. She and Mandy exchange exasperated glances.

'Stop fucking ganging up on me, you slags,' says me and we get back to our soup in silence.

We pay up and walk outside. A man selling postcards and an old woman selling cigarettes pounce on us. I growl at them but then relent and buy a pack of fags for the first time in weeks. I open the shiny new pack, in awe at its ordered cleanliness, and sit on a bench for a minute feeling the stress melting away in a fetid haze of head rush and oxygen deprivation.

'Fuck... sorry Lucy,' I purr, rejoining the girls outside yet another Alpaca boutique. 'Sorry Mandy. I just get so fucking stressed out in these tourist traps, you know? I just hate being treated like a sucker.'

'You are a sucker,' says Lucy, but there's humour in her bonny Scotch eye.

'Fuck you,' I grin, 'and fuck you too, Mandy Stowe,' grabbing her in a bear hug and squeezing her arse.

A smiling 'Fook off Stinky!' is the inevitable response.

We wander into a tourist office and politely inquire about train tickets and prices. Like the goofy bastard gringos we are, we ask stupid questions like:

'How far in miles is the track? How steep is it? Are there lots of bridges? Is it dangerous?'

They presume we're just dumb tourists asking dumb tourist questions, but that's where they're wrong, that's where they're the goofy bastards, because we're a highly trained squad of must-see bandits on a mother fucking must-see mission.

We fall in outside. I light another fag.

'This is shit,' I observe constructively. 'We'll never make it up twenty miles of fucking train track before morning at this altitude. Especially not with your asthma, Lucy and your... fucking you Mandy. Who the fuck told you it was only eighteen clicks anyway?'

'Some guy I met in Colombia,' says Lucy. 'He said he'd walked it. He was a wee bit of a cock though.'

'Great, fucking great.'

'So are we not going to Machu Picchu then?' asks Mandy.

Lucy and I look at each other, both realising that just enough of an obstacle has been placed in our path for us to retire with some dignity.

'Fuck no!' we chorus.

'Let's go to the pub then,' says Mandy.

'Okay.' And we do.

Some hours later I'm sitting on a stone stairway overlooking the lights of Cuzco. I'm crying. Lucy is sitting next to me. She's crying too.

Lucy is crying about her ovaries. Mandy is back at the hostel, crying because I told her that Lucy's ovaries were more important than her whinging. I said that because I'm drunk. In fact I'm crying because I'm drunk, because of Lucy's ovaries, because of Mandy's whinging and because of John Peel.

'What a place to go, eh John?' I say to Cuzco below. 'What a fucking shite hole.'

And we cry. Tears plopping into the dust and dried llama shit, sunken tears of weakness, drunken tears of woe.

16: Titicaca (Willy don't serf)

With heavy bags and diarrhoea, with dusty shoes and straining lungs, with frayed tempers and things unsaid, we leave Cuzco behind. Onto a crowded bus we flop, where a fuzzy TV is showing a badly dubbed Van Damme movie. Jean Claude, as is his wont, is co-starring alongside himself, kicking his own arse so to speak. The Peruvian passengers are hooked, agape at supple roundhouses and splattering blood. Outside their windows nature has once again made herself beautiful, with snow capped peaks in the distance and horses on the plains, with eagles in the air and the dusty sun an orange globe among the wispy clouds. It seems to scream at me from my peripheral vision every time my eyes wander to the screen:

'Look, human, look how pretty I am. Look at my subtle curves and rusty peaks. Look at my damp hollows and mossy recesses. Loook. Loooook.'

Like Ulysses tied to the mast, I cannot resist. I listen, I look and I love. The Peruvians, parsley in their ears, brown hands tied to their oars, are oblivious. I understand, for many years ago I too felt the allure of that same supple master, I too felt the pull of that most Belgian of dwarves. In Peru, on this bus, nature has taken on the might of Van Damme and nature has lost.

Upon the shores of that vast sea of grass we come upon a town. It is a dry, brutish place, a sprawling mass of rusted scrap yards and angry looking locals. Mandy, Lucy and I exchange nervous looks, hoping beyond hope that this isn't our final stop. Praying that we don't have to get out in this nasty shite hole and find a place to stay among the railways tracks and mangy dogs. We are weary, you see, weary of high altitude towns and filth, weary of dust and scrawny kids, weary of Peru.

This time we are in luck though. The bus starts up again in a cloud of blue-black exhaust and we begin to roll and bounce out of town.

But just as we think we're clear, just as we leave behind the last crusty dwelling there comes a yelling and a bawling from the back, the bus screeches to a halt and an argument ensues. A funny-looking white man is yelling at the driver, the driver is yelling at the co-driver/bag-man and the co-driver/bag-man is looking confused and sorry for himself. I make out enough of what they're saying to realise that the white man's son has been left behind in Rusty-Shitsville. The white man is very unhappy to have lost his son. The co-driver/bag-man is also very unhappy. The driver doesn't seem to care.

But this deadlocked situation is quickly rectified when the funny-looking white man's funny-looking son arrives in a taxi with a bag of oranges and everyone gets back onto the bus and we trundle on along the dusty old road. He may not seem very important now, but remember that funny-looking white man's funny-looking son; he is important in the future, wait...

Titicaca. I've been dimly aware of it since I was a kid. It's one of those places, like Timbuktu or Zanzibar, which you don't really believe exists. How could it? How could anywhere with a name like that really exist?

Well it does, look, behind that red outcrop there, behind those fields of rustling reeds, like a polished mirror reflecting the sky, there it is. 'The highest navigable lake on earth' is what it is. A weird claim to fame it seems to me, like those giant papier-mâché sculptures on the outskirts of small Australian towns: 'the biggest corn-cob in the world' or 'the world's largest banana', a pointlessly specific claim to fame.

Into the town of Puno we now roll, we three, our bones and bums sore from the road and the Imodium, our eyes and minds tired from the view and the daydreaming. It isn't Cuzco, this town, but it would like to be. It wants the tourists and their dollars, it really does.

We make camp in a new, nearly empty, five-storey backpacker hostel and sleep like dogs, Mandy and I rolling and tangling in our double bed, the new neon sign buzzing outside our window, Lucy alone in her single room.

The next day, for the first time in South America, we decide to take a guided tour. For months I've resisted, I've argued and I've refused, but after the Machu Picchu fiasco I feel I owe the girls a concession, perhaps I even owe myself a concession, and so I concede.

This is how we find ourselves on a small boat rustling through the reeds, navigating the highest navigable lake in the world. We are welcomed aboard in four different languages and sit politely among our fellow Caucasians and exchange greetings and shy nods. I hate it already. The Germans on board are talking very loudly to each other and ignoring everyone else, the North Americans are just pleased as punch to be here and are taking too many pictures, the weird-looking French couple over there, are just staring absentmindedly over the stern. The Welsh, who don't like guided tours, have climbed onto the roof of the cabin to smoke fags and try not to be too much of a downer for everyone else.

It is pretty though, the endless sky, the billowing high-altitude clouds so close to the mountains, the hiss of the hull against the reeds. I lie back, close my eyes and try to ignore the multilingual prattle from the cabin. When I open them the tall, bearded man whose nationality I couldn't place is sitting next to me.

'G'day,' he says to me.

'Hey,' I say back.

His name is Hamish and I like him immediately. He's a Kiwi who's been living in Venezuela for a while. His folks have come out from New Zealand to visit him. They're 'doing' Titicaca. We talk about Chavez and Venezuela for a while. Then his old man comes up and we talk about fishing and altitude and they tell me stories of sailing trips on the Tasman and the Pacific. They plainly love each other, father and son, and I like that too, it gives me a pleasant twinge of homesickness.

The first stop on our guided tour is a floating island of reeds made by an Indian tribe who have bobbed on this lake for generations. We jump ashore and gather round a small exhibition of fish, cooking pots, crafts and local indigenous types. Our guide expounds at great length in English, French, German and Spanish about how the Indians came down from the hills, persecuted by Incas and other warring tribes, and settled on the lake. I watch the four shawled Indian women as he speaks, imagining what it must have taken to push people to pile reeds upon reeds and float out to the safety of the lake. The guide tells us that there are many such islands on Titicaca, that they are semi-autonomous, with their own leaders and customs, that they eat only what the lake provides and live all year round on their fishy islands.

When he is done expounding, an Indian in a colourful, woolly hat appears in a huge canoe of reeds with a great gaping figurehead. Some of us climb aboard to be ferried to a neighbouring island while the others take the tour boat.

Hamish and I chat to the Indian oarsman while he digs and strains at his work, like a pintsize gondolier. He tells us that life is fine on the lake, that they make lots of money these days. He tells us that the islands on which the Indians live are very different from the ones that the tourists see. He tells us that his canoe is made of a reed skeleton full of plastic Coca-Cola bottles, that this adds five years to the life of the canoe. On an island in the distance I can see cosy looking houses of wood and a speedboat hidden in the reeds, yet on the islands we visit there are only damp little huts and wicker canoes. His canoe, I imagine, is very much like the lake people's lives: modern living dressed up in ancient clothes.

As the day turns to evening we land on a long island of rock and earth and pile out of the boat, glad to be ashore among the sheep and wildflowers. Our welcoming committee stands in a semicircle on the quay grinning endearingly at us. A hollow feeling in my guts yawns and stirs at the sight of them. There are perhaps twenty of them, middle aged men and women, all dressed in the Peruvian national costume. The men, their faces tanned and weather beaten, all wear white shirts, black trousers and waistcoats, bowler hats and brightly coloured cummerbunds. The women, their jet-black hair tied in neat plaits, wear huge puffy skirts, bright shawls and, like the men, small grey or black bowler hats.

We stand around in groups in front of the committee and our guide calls out our names, pairing us up with Indian couples who, he explains, will be our mother and father for the night. Mandy, Lucy and I are the last group to be placed. I watch the other tourists' reactions as they are led away, to see if they too feel the same odd panic which is rising in me, but they just quietly follow their new mums and dads, looking slightly bemused.

Then we are introduced to our new parents, a handsome, gnarled man and his rosy-cheeked wife. As I shake their hands I try to read their faces, try to see if there is any appreciation of the strangeness of this situation, but I can read nothing in their black eyes, their carved mouths.

We follow them up a wide stony path between awkward-looking fields and tethered donkeys to a little stone cottage. They show us to a small, comfortable room and we sit outside and look over the lake to the distant peaks of Bolivia and the little islands in between. While we talk quietly and smoke, our new mum stumbles shyly up to us with an armful of home-knit alpaca scarves and socks. We admire them and, motivated almost entirely by the embarrassed look on her dark face, we buy as much as we can afford without haggling at all. By the time she bows and shuffles off to the smoky little kitchen below I am squirming with embarrassment. I feel like some ghastly lord of the manor imposing myself on my grovelling serfs.

This is not how I immerse myself in foreign cultures: with guilt and shame, with awkwardness, and a hollow rattling in my soul.

The sky begins to redden in the west and we settle down in the candlelight to read and softly whinge to one another. But the fun isn't over yet. Our new mother and giggling little sister appear with armfuls of Peruvian national dress clothes. We try to explain that we're tired but they insist that we must dress up because there is to be a party tonight in our honour. So, entering into the spirit of things as much as we can, we don our musty costumes and follow Papa out into the night, towards the village hall.

The door to the hall is open and yellow light streams out, illuminating groups of gringos in bowlers and ponchos standing around outside. We make our way into the crowded room and sit down on the chairs which hug the walls. It looks like a school disco. At both ends of the long hall wooden platforms have been erected on which two bands will take turns to play, like some kind of ancient sound clash. An image pops into my head of what it would be like if my community in Wales had to dress in national costume and dance for the tourists and I shudder. Then Hamish appears next to me looking like an Afghan fighter with his beard and poncho. I see straight away that he feels as uncomfortable as I do with the scene, but there's no time to talk, the band begins in earnest, banging out Simon and Garfunkel panpipe stomps, without the moles and holes, and we're dragged to our feet by local girls who look bored and duty-bound to dance with us. They avoid eye contact and whirl us around until we can't breathe. But they won't let us go so we go on dancing for politeness' sake, until it seems that we're all just keeping up a thin façade.

Most of the other guests don't seem to see it that way though, most of them seem happy enough. I hear them waffling about how enchanting village life is and how special it is to see some real culture instead of the modern living of the townsfolk.

I find Hamish flopped on a chair fighting off a villager. He says his parents couldn't face it. I sit down and we watch the grim, whirling faces of the locals, politely refusing dances and smiling when we're smiled at, but I'm squirming inside. I can stand it no more.

'This is killing me,' I say quietly.

He turns and looks me evenly in the eye.

'They do this every night, you know?' he says. 'This is their job. You're not doing them any harm.'

'So far today,' I reply, 'I've parted with more money than the average Peruvian makes in a month. Yet the people I'm staying with live without electricity and running water. Either they've got another house with a satellite dish and a Playstation on the other side of the island or something isn't quite right.'

'These people are here to provide an entertaining illusion for the tourists, Wil. It's a Peruvian Disneyland, don't take it so seriously.'

I nod and I know I shouldn't, but that emptiness in my gut is still gnawing away at me.

Hamish continues: 'That's just how business is done in Peru, it seems underhand and fake to us but you have to let it go, otherwise you'll be consumed by it.'

'I can't, you know,' I say sadly.

That night Hamish told me a story. He had been trekking in a remote part of the Peruvian Andes. With him were some other westerners he didn't know and four Peruvian guides, one of them just a boy. For several days the Peruvians guided them along the mountain tracks and barren places, through deep snow and forests, through thin air and rain. On the fifth day, in a very wild and desolate place, they came upon a man in rags huddled by the wayside. The man was Peruvian. He said he hadn't eaten or drunk anything for a long time. He said he was very cold and very hungry.

'*Tengo mucho hambre, Señor,*' he said. '*Soy mucho frió.*'

Hamish took off his pack and took from it his spare warm jacket, some water and a little food.

'This man needs help', he said to the rest of the group, and he wrapped the warm jacket about the man's shivering shoulders, gave him some food and a little water.

'But we have to keep on with our trekking,' said one of the white men. The others nodded sternly.

'He is going to die, *Señor*,' said one of the guides and they nodded too.

'But I must help him,' said Hamish, 'he is not dead yet.'

The guides shrugged.

'It will cost you more money,' one of them said. 'We must have a horse to carry him.'

'So I will hire a horse.'

'But we must carry on with our trekking.' The others nodded again.

'So go,' said Hamish to the westerners, 'take two guides and I will hire a horse and take this man to a village where he can see a doctor.'

'That is good,' said the white man, 'we will do that.'

'Wait,' said one of the guides, 'you will need more than two guides. Who will carry the cooking pots and food? Who will carry the big tents and water bottles? You will need more than two guides.'

'So I will hire more guides,' said Hamish. 'This man needs my help and so I shall help him.'

And so it was that the boy was sent to a village to find a horse and more guides. When they returned the westerners said goodbye to Hamish and walked away, leaving him with two new guides and the boy, the dying man and the horse.

'Good,' said Hamish when they had secured the man in the saddle. 'Now we can find a doctor.'

'The doctor is very far away, *Señor*,' said one of the new guides.

'But we will take you to him,' said the other, and they all set off slowly down the mountain.

As the day wore on the dying man started to look much happier, snug as he was in Hamish's warm jacket, with food and water in his belly. When they came to a steep place one of the guides said: 'This place is very dangerous for the horse, *Señor*, you take this short cut and we will go another way.'

The other guide pointed to a boulder at the bottom of the

valley and said: 'that is where our paths will meet again.'

So Hamish walked down the steep path. The two guides and the boy, the dying man and the horse took another path. Among the boulders of the valley floor they met again. From their faces and the way they held their shoulders Hamish knew that something was wrong.

'What is the matter?' he asked the boy, but the boy only looked at the ground and said nothing.

'What is the matter?' he asked the guides.

'The man is dead,' they said and their faces were as hard as stone. 'He died when you were on the other path. We could do nothing for him.'

'But he looked better,' said Hamish. 'He looked much better.'

The guides only shrugged and said, 'He is dead now.'

Hamish turned to the boy. 'How is it that he was happy and now he is dead?' But the boy would not answer. He would not even look at Hamish.

'This is bad,' said Hamish.

'Yes it is bad,' said the guides. 'Now we will have to go to the police station and you will have to speak to the police. It is very far and it will cost you more money.'

I do not want to go to the police station, thought Hamish, *I do not trust these guides. I do not like the way they look at me. I do not like the way the boy does not look at me. I am very far from any help and I do not feel safe.*

'You go to the police with him,' said Hamish, 'and I will try to catch up with my friends. Maybe the boy can show me the way.'

'No!' said the guides angrily, 'You must come with us. You must not go with the boy back into the mountains.'

I am bigger than they are, thought Hamish and he was scared, *but they are small and strong and there are two of them.*

I must get away from here quickly or this will be bad for me.

'I shall go by myself then,' said Hamish bravely and he quickly walked back the way he had come.

'No!' they said, and started after him. 'You must not go alone. You must come with us to the police. You must pay us for our guiding and our horse.'

'No,' said Hamish over his shoulder as he hurried away. 'I have paid for the horse and I have paid for your guiding. I will pay you no more.'

Behind him he could hear them arguing and shouting and he hurried on, taking only the steepest paths so that they could not follow him with the horse. For hours Hamish walked, afraid that he was being followed by the men. When it started to rain he kept walking and when darkness fell he walked still. He had no torch and it was very dark and very cold. When he lost the path he used the little light on his wristwatch to find his way and when he could walk no more he climbed into his wet sleeping bag with his boots on and slept in the shelter of an overhanging boulder.

When the milky light of dawn came Hamish began to walk again. He was high up in the mountains and he had eaten nothing but a chocolate bar in twenty-four hours. He was very cold and very light headed. Hamish walked and walked until early afternoon. By now it was very bad for him. He stumbled along very slowly and his mind was numb and far away. He knew that he couldn't last much longer, but he knew he had to try. And then Hamish had the first piece of luck he'd had in days. A French couple who were trekking the same high, ragged hills came upon him huddled by the wayside.

'Are you okay?' they asked. 'You look like you need some help.' And they opened their packs and gave Hamish dry clothes and food and they got out their camping stove and made him a nice cup of tea to warm him inside.

'Thank you,' he said, 'thank you for helping me.'

And the three of them walked off the mountain together.

I look about at the people around me, the whirling skirts and flying hair, the pale skin of the gringos and the dark faces of the locals, and I try to imagine what they're thinking. But as always their eyes tell me nothing, their faces set, emotions locked deep within.

'Jesus...' I sigh, rubbing my eyes to get rid of the dark thoughts. 'That's some story. Did you ever get your jacket back?'

'No.' Hamish smiles, 'No I didn't.'

I leave the party soon afterwards, still in my poncho and hat, and wander through the darkness towards our little cottage. The moon is up and shining pale and silver on the lake. Over on the Bolivian shore a thunder storm is silently pounding the snowy peaks. Lightning exposes the jagged silhouette of the Andes in quick bursts, but it's too far off to hear thunder.

I sit on a boulder beside a little grove of yellow-flowered shrubs and watch the flashing clouds. I feel like crying again. I feel dirty inside somehow and it hurts. A figure comes towards me along the path, black against the light of the party, music and voices drifting over the fields before it. It is our surrogate father-for-the-night.

'¿Todo bien?' He hails me.

'Si,' I call back, trying to make it sound cheerful. 'Todo bien, Señor.'

He says he'd been waiting for me, to show me the way home, and I say the moon is fine and I know the way, but thanks anyway. He sits down next to me and I offer him a cigarette and he takes one and eyes it with admiration before lighting it, his gnarled face suddenly a flickering orange disc in the light of the match and then black again as he blows it out. I ask him if I can ask him something personal and he grunts a yes, so I ask him if he enjoys what he does.

'We are not hungry,' he says simply, in Spanish. 'There are many hungry people out there,' he sweeps his arm across the distant mainland. 'We have food.'

We sit quietly, smoking and watching the lightning move slowly northwards.

'Where I grew up,' I say to him, 'we have many tourists in the summer. They come with new cars and expensive clothes to walk in the mountains. We always hated them when we were kids.'

I suppose I'm trying to find some common ground with him, to see if he'll open up at all, but he listens in silence and then he stubs his cigarette out in a shower of little orange sparks and we quietly walk back to the cottage together.

I lie in bed with Mandy breathing softly beside me, and stay awake for a long time, thinking it all over. I realise that I am angry. Really angry. That gnawing hole in my stomach is not embarrassment, it is not shame or resentment, it is rage. Rage at the injustice of it all, the starving kids, the rotten lives of the many made a hundred times more rotten by the greed of the few. Rage at myself and my kind, at our inability to see beyond our safe little bubbles, at our misplaced, patronising empathy, at our conceit and at our lofty self image. And again I cry, sobbing quietly, my whole body clenched, my eyes shut tight, my stomach shaking. Tears of boiling rage and frustration I cry, and they run in hot lines down my cheeks and into my pillow. And then, after a while, I sleep.

17: La Paz

A few days later, at a nondescript border crossing, we kiss Peru a tearless farewell. It's like saying goodbye to a guest who's overstayed his welcome, a guest who wasn't really welcome in the first place but who stayed anyway, cramping our personal space and treading dirt into the clean carpets of our souls. I am not sad to be leaving. Nor am I sad to have been. I am just sad, sad and weary.

Our first taste of Bolivia is Casa Blanca, a little town of whitewashed houses scattered on the shores of Titicaca. It took us hours to get here yet it looks almost exactly like the Peruvian town we left this morning. We could have been driving in circles.

In a courtyard café we sit, and drink sweet black coffee among the climbing roses and honeysuckle. We are all a bit sad today, frowning and tight mouthed. We talk glumly, half-heartedly, about plans and strategies, but we're not really saying anything.

'I know!' I say after a few minutes of swapping sullen jibes with Lucy and staring into my coffee cup. 'Let's drop the last of the Bromazipam and get the next bus to La Paz, clean ourselves up and go to a bar and get pissed. There's no point staying here. Let's just keep moving.'

The girls smile and nod weakly, like sick kids offered ice cream. So with bellies full of Brommies to mellow the mood and the welcome thought of a little civilisation up ahead, we leave Casa Blanca...

La Paz. The peace. Why they call it that I have no idea. It looks like a landslide – a glacier of tarmac, concrete and metal cascading haphazardly down a steep valley. The outskirts of the city – dusty mud-brick dwellings and rusting gas stations, turn slowly into cratered streets and dirty, five storey buildings. Pigeon shit lintels and scrawny dogs. There are people everywhere: Cholos in ponchos, businessmen in shiny suits, green uniformed soldiers and shawled, vicious-looking old ladies, shoeshine boys in balaclavas and traffic cops in pith helmets and white gloves.

It is a high, cold city, loud and busy; from the barrios on the hillsides to the witches' market in the valley, it is crazy and intense. And above it all and always in sight, like a colossal fang in the crooked and broken jaw of the Andes, Mt Illimani towers, its pure, white majesty quietly accentuating the crumbling decrepitude of the city, shaming it, keeping it in its place.

We find ourselves, packs on the pavement, shivering in the cold wind. With fuzzy, cotton wool brains from the Bromazipam and the altitude we flag down a cab and hurtle from hostel to hostel, only to be informed at every one that there are no rooms available. It is a strangely familiar scene.

We want comfort, we want civility and civilisation. We want hot baths and clean beds. But there just aren't enough to go round and we've turned up too late.

This déjà vu nativity scene carries on a while; our morale sinks lower and lower each time we are turned away, until we come upon a hostel that still has rooms available. A hostel, not a love hotel, with clean beds and hot water, yet a hostel whose outward appearance leaves us in no doubt as to why it is nearly empty when all the others are full. It is a huge and ruinous place, an ancient and seedy pile of mildewed arches and mouldy stairways, of old graffiti and dank, cat piss corners.

Even the taxi driver doesn't think we should stay here. He doesn't think we should even be in the neighbourhood. But we are tired, tired and unable to make any decisions for ourselves, so we trust in fate and pay the fare and the cabbie watches us stumble down the narrow, cobbled alley to a wooden door above which is written 'Hosbitaje Del Muerte', or words to that effect.

Under the stairs in the courtyard, in a filthy cupboard of a room, sits a strange man. He is Peruvian. His long, black hair, colourful poncho and black-brown eyes give that much away instantly. He is short and thick and his eyes are red and vague, but not without intensity. On a stool outside his room sits another strange man. He is North American. His long, blond hair and beard, his carefully bohemian clothes, his freckled, delicate fingers and his accent give that away. They are sharing a large bottle of beer and listening to *The White Album* on a small portable CD player. It jumps and skips incessantly.

'Hey,' I say, lazily, bohemianly, phonetically: 'Haay.'

'*¿Que pasa?*' says the Yank, equally lazily. The Peruvian says nothing. He just watches me with eyes shot through with shattered capillaries.

'Mind if I sit?' I ask the Yank in English, my eyes on the Peruvian. My body language and tone says: 'I mean you no harm.'

'Ain't up to me man,' says the Yank.

I nod and sit down anyway, taking a pack of cigarettes slowly from my pocket and offering them around. The Peruvian looks at me for a long time, then he seems to make up his mind and takes one. We sit and smoke and say nothing, the Yank nods his head constantly as if he is agreeing with something only he can hear, his eyes half closed. The Peruvian sits on his unmade bed and rocks slightly, watching me the whole time. I sit with my legs crossed and blow smoke out of my nose, squinting at the Yank and then at the Peruvian, at the wilted potted plants in the courtyard and the little square of sky high above while McCartney stammers and stutters in the background: 'ob-ob-ob-ob-obla-bla-obladee'.

'Hey listen,' I say to the Yank after a while, 'd'you know where I can score some weed?'

'Huh?' He says. 'Mmmm,' and he points a bony finger at the Peruvian who thrusts his jaw out at me.

'*Amigo*,' I say, '*necesito comprar poco verde para fumar.*'

It is bad Spanish, just a direct translation of what I'd say in English.

'Mmmm,' he says and does this thing with his head that isn't a nod or a shake.

'Mmmm,' I say too and decide to drop it for now.

'Hey, where you *from*, man?' asks the Yank.

'Wales.'

The Yank's face lights up. '*Wales*, man?' He says.

'Uh-huh.'

'Far fucking *out*,' he says without explanation and he goes back to nodding agreements to his inner voices.

'*¿Que dice?*' asks the Peruvian.

'Oh,' I say, a bit confused. '*Nada. Solamente soy Gales. Nada mas.*'

'*¿Que?*' he asks again, his eyes narrow, vicious slits.

'*Nana amigo, tranquilo,*' I say quickly, turning to the Yank. 'Hey, I wasn't saying nothing bad, man. Tell him I didn't mean to say anything bad.'

'Mmmm,' he says, nodding, 'it's okay man. Everything's fine.'

I shut my mouth and sit back; the Peruvian's eyes are still vicious, still watching me. He mutters something under his breath and starts rocking again. I reach for my ciggies and offer him one but this time he just scowls and shakes his head. The Yank takes one, smiling and nodding at me.

'I'm going to get some beer,' I say, standing up. 'Can I get you guys anything?'

I walk out into the night feeling like something's come

adrift somewhere, like reality hasn't been behaving itself quite as it should.

Maybe I should have gone shopping with Lucy and Mandy, I think, but I'm glad I didn't. We've spent way too much time in each other's company and I need this time away from them, however strange it's turning out to be.

Fuck I need a reefer. I pull my hood up and my cap down and do the Shaolin strut past a mess of bums and junkies collected in the shadow of a doorway. The nearest shop is just up the cobbled lane; a doorway of yellow light cutting across the alley, an old woman behind a worn, wooden counter with a lazy eye and shelves of dust and rice and beer.

'*Tres cervezas grande por favor, señora,*' I say, looking at her in what I think is her good eye. '*Y una caje de cigarillos, gracias.*'

Then I wander slowly back the way I came trying to work out what exactly it is I'm wandering back into. One of the bums in the alley catches my eye. I look back at him blankly, without fear or hostility. He nods once, respectfully, and I raise my chin and purse my lips at him like they do in Venezuela. I pass and that is that. And that tiny exchange makes me feel better. Even if reality is flailing around like a skink's lost tail I can still ride it, I can still be me. I shrug and sigh and step back into the crummy hostel doorway.

They are sitting as I'd left them, the Yank nodding and smiling at nothing, the Peruvian hunched and scowling.

You could shut yourself up in the room and drink these you know, Willy. I say to myself, but I know I won't, I know I'd rather be part of this weird scene and maybe smoke a joint than sit and read and drink alone.

'Hey,' I say again by way of greeting. But this time, because of the bum in the alley, my body language and tone says: 'I mean no harm, but I mean to take none either.' I sit down and pop the cap off one of the beers with my lighter, swig a mouthful and offer the bottle to the Peruvian. He takes it, more out of greed than camaraderie, sucks it back and hands it to the Yank. The Beatles are still skipping and jumping in the background. I find myself thinking about Charlie Manson and just for a second I feel oddly close to him.

'Where are you from?' I ask the Yank, to get that leering, swastika'd face out of mind.

'Montana,' he says and I nod.

'My name's Wil, by the way,' I say and hold out my hand. He lets it hang there for a couple of seconds and then takes it, saying:

'Jed.'

I turn to the Peruvian and we shake hands too. His name is Cesar. Mine is Wil, Wil 'I'd love it if you could stop being so weird and give me a joint' Gritten.

But the world just doesn't work like that. This is how it works: We sit and nod and share my beer and cigarettes and listen to Lennon's bad trip. Then Lucy and Mandy turn up from the shops or wherever they've been and they join our little circle of gross abstraction long enough to never want to come back. The Peruvian leers and pants. The Yank smiles and nods. Nobody says anything.

'Er... can I have a word Wil?' Says Mandy. I nod, force a smile and we move out of earshot leaving poor Lucy behind.

'Who the fook are *they*?' She nods towards the Peruvian under the stairs and the Yank with the weeble head.

'Just some dudes,' I say and I catch a note in my voice which I realise with disbelief is defensiveness. I cringe at myself. 'I didn't fancy drinking by myself in the room. I'm trying to get some weed from them,' and I put my arms around her. 'They're fucking weird, man.'

She kisses me and I feel like I could just cuddle up with

her under the bed clothes and hide forever.

'We were thinking of getting some coke from this guy at reception,' she says. 'D'you want to put in?'

'Sure,' I say, trying to snap out of my instinctive need to hibernate. 'Yeah, um, get Lucy away from them and I'll get some cash.'

I know I shouldn't really be doing it, but I fish out my money belt from under the bed and pull out a wad of Bolivianos and stuff them in my pocket.

'Those guys are fucking *weird*,' Lucy says behind me. Again I feel the muscles in my shoulders tense defensively and again I wonder at myself.

What's wrong with me? I'm so uptight.

I shrug, hand her the cash and tell her to be careful and not get ripped off. She gives me a look and Mandy gives me a wink and they leave. For a while I stand where they left me and look after them. Then I shrug again and leave too.

Three hours go by. We'd split the bag of yellowish crystals into lines on the cover of a paperback edition of Walden and hoovered them into our faces with rolled up hundreds. Our faces had turned instantly numb and our heart rates had doubled. 'Jesus,' we'd said in wonder and immediately begun to chew each other's ears off, talking very, very fast.

I left Lucy and Mandy discussing their insecurities and sallied forth to find a reefer. Now I'm back with the people under the stairs. Little has changed in the scene apart from the CD and the amount of burst capillaries in the Peruvian's eyes. I have changed though. I no longer feel that my grip on reality is slipping. I feel like I've willingly let go and I can easily climb this thing without handholds. I am riding a white horse down the greased helter-skelter of the world and that's okay, man, that's just fine.

I down again, making a mental note not to talk too much or chew my face.

'Hey,' I say, and this time I say it just right.

'Mmmm,' nods Jed.

'*Hola*,' says Cesar warmly.

I hadn't expected that.

'*Hola*,' I say back and accept the beer he offers.

'Where are you from?' he asks in Spanish.

'Wales,' I answer, in Spanish.

'Where's that?'

So I give him the same geography lesson I've given a million times before and he gives the same response as everyone else:

'So it's in England then?' I try not to talk too fast or be too enthusiastic when I tell him that no, it's a different country with a different language and a different culture, much older than the English, and I wonder why he suddenly wants to be my friend. Then he asks me:

'Where are the chicas?' and now I know.

The night is cold and in the small square of night sky above the courtyard stars flicker and twinkle, the drone of traffic continues ceaselessly from the highway. We sit and drink and I talk at a hundred miles an hour, the wind in my hair, life whizzing by like tracer bullets. We are talking about politics. Jed is quiet. Cesar is crying.

'They took my brother from me,' he sobs. 'They took him from me and they killed him.'

'Who?' I ask, not sure if I've even understood him.

'The military,' his eyes blaze viciously again. 'The son of a whore military and the son of a whore government.'

I'm listening at a hundred miles an hour now, coming in low and fast over the sound, snatching at it even as it's made. I force a nod for normality's sake.

'He was a guerrilla,' the sounds that Cesar makes say. 'He

was on the Shining Path and they took him, tortured and...
killed him.' Great tears, like lumps of amber, roll down his
brown cheeks.

'Is that why you're here, under the stairs?' I ask, licking
my lips too fast.

'*Si*,' he says bitterly, throws his head back and launches
half a bottle of beer into his mouth.

'I'm sorry for your troubles,' I say. Then I raise my right
arm, fist clenched and, because I've always wanted to say it
in context, I say:

'*¡Viva la revolution!*'

Cesar just cries harder and I sit and chew my face, the
synapses of my mind popping and fizzing like tiny fireworks
at a million miles an hour. Jed just goes on nodding.

18: Max (a lot of eights)

In a bar in downtown La Paz we sit, on comfy, clean seats,
White Russians on the low glass table in front of us. We talk
with exaggerated enthusiasm about things we forget as quickly
as we think of them. It's good to be in here, good to be warm
and comfortable and away from the madness of the last few
days. Good to feel civilised, even if that feeling is largely down
to the Devil's Dandruff.

'I'll get these,' I say, like the big, generous patriarch.

Their rosy faces beam up at me and I skip happily upstairs
to the bar to get the bill and maybe have a little flirt with the
waitress.

Upstairs is quieter now. It's almost three. Just a few
couples at the bar and a group of Israelis at a table. The staff
are looking out at the street through the big plate-glass
window. The barman is drying a glass with a tea towel. I put

both hands on the bar and follow his gaze. Outside a lone gringo is talking to a small, dark man beside a parked car.

'¿Que pasa?' I ask, friendly, enthusiastic.

'That guy out there is a bad man,' the barman answers in Spanish.

'We're worried about that gringo,' says the waitress.

I wander over to the window and look out. The gold-leaf lettering is peeling a little. The night looks cold and dangerous. I look at the gringo.

'Oh shit, I know that guy,' I say, and I do. It's that odd-looking guy's odd-looking son who the bus driver tried to maroon on the way to Titicaca. 'What's wrong with the other one?'

'He is trouble, *Señor*,' the barman says gravely. 'He has been giving people a lot of trouble around here lately.'

I look back out the window. He doesn't look too bad to me, short and wiry, probably carries a knife. My thinking is too fast, too rash, too much up my nose and not enough in my guts.

'I'll go and see if he's okay.' I open the door and I'm out in the cold air before they can say anything. The gringo and the *hombre mal* are standing very close to each other. When I cross the road I see that they're sharing a crack pipe.

He looks like he's handling himself well enough to me, I think and I would usually have walked away at that point, knowing that the gringo wasn't about to be stabbed or mugged, but my brain is quick and numb so I just walk right up to them.

'Hey!' I say to the gringo, grinning like a chimp. 'Remember me? I was there when your arse nearly got left behind in that shitty Hicksville town in Peru.'

He just stands there looking at me, blinking. The other man does the same.

'Why don't you come and have a drink with me and my

friends,' I say and put my hand on his shoulder. He looks at my hand, confused, and then smiles.

'I do not speak English,' he says in a thick accent.

'Fuck,' is all I can think to say.

'Where you *from* man?' says the other man, the *hombre mal*, in a thick New York accent.

'Jesus,' is all I can think to say.

'You okay, dude?' he asks me, and offers me the burnt-brown crack pipe. 'Blaze?'

'No,' I say, then I remember my manners. 'No thanks man,' and I smile. 'Where are *you* from?'

'East New York born and bred,' he says, holding his arms wide as if to embrace my congratulations. His face is young, almost innocent, but his eyes are fast and mean. A scar like a slipped hair lip pulls down the corner of his mouth, his clothes are grubby and worn.

'What are you doing here?' I ask. 'I had you down for a mugger, man. So did the people in that bar I was in.'

We look over at the bar; the staff are still watching us, the barman with his tea towel in his hand.

'I got busted,' he says. 'I was eighteen. Trying to move eight keys of puro back into the States. They gave me eight years.'

'Sheesh.' I raise my eyebrows. 'That's a lot of eights.'

'Huh,' he says and grins at me.

'Huh,' I say and grin back.

The odd-looking dude is still standing beside us looking confused, but he's smiling too.

'Name's Wil,' I say and hold out my hand.

'Max,' he says and gives me that NY handshake thing I was always a bit awkward with. The waitress scratches her chin and looks worriedly out at us.

'His name's Paulo,' Max points at Odd-guy with his

thumb, 'but he don't understand English 'cos he's Brazilian.'

I nod and smile. 'You know, Max,' I turn back to him, 'you just blew my mind when you turned round and asked me where I was from. I nearly lost it.'

'Happens all the time,' says Max proudly.

'You know, you don't look too bad for having just done eight years in a Bolivian nick,' I say, with admiration rather than disbelief.

'You don't think, eh?' And he lifts his shirt. His stomach is a mess of interlocking scar tissue, a bad mess.

'Fuck,' I say, but we're still grinning at each other.

'Are you heading back to the States soon?' I ask.

'Na man! Are you crazy?' And he's laughing happily. 'When I can sell to the gringos at ten times the price and live like a king? Hell, even if I do get busted twenny bucks buys me out the same night. I'd be crazy not to stay, man.'

I laugh but I heard a little hollow note in his voice when he said it.

'I rap too,' he says, making triggers with his index fingers. 'You wanna hear my shit?'

'I don't even need to, Max,' I shake my head in slow, wondering admiration. 'I don't even need to.'

I wander back over the road still shaking my head. The girls are waiting for me and the staff don't make eye contact. I pay the bill and put on my jacket.

'He's okay,' I say to the barman

But the barman doesn't care so I say goodnight and follow the girls outside.

On the way home I tell them enthusiastically about my meeting with Max.

'He was almost completely wild,' I say, like I'm talking about a fox cub. 'He was all that hip hop bollocks personified but he was entirely real.'

They look at me with complete bewilderment. I suddenly realise that in their eyes I'm getting excited about meeting a maniac with no redeeming feature other than a crack habit. But there was something about Max, his enthusiasm, the good in him bubbling just below the surface. I try to explain it to the girls but it's no use, so I shut up and we wander quietly home, home to the hostel of death and the people under the stairs.

I'm getting to be as bad as Linden Dewey, I think to myself. *Life's getting a bit weird. I'm going to need a holiday soon.*

19: Tupiza

I left town and walked south along the old railway. I needed to escape, needed to get away from Mandy and Lucy, needed time on my own, just me and the canyon, the snakes and the cacti.

It's so quiet the gulp of the water going down my throat and the crackle of the plastic bottle echo down the valley, the rattle of small pebbles dislodged by my dirty trainers is crisp and clear.

With a bandana over my mouth and nose and dust already settling on my clothes I struck west up a dry creek bed. In a thicket I cut myself a metre of green bamboo cane and punctured my hand on a bush of long, black thorns. The red blood oozed out and clotted almost immediately in the hot, dry air, like round, red beads on the white skin of my palm.

Soon I left the mud brick houses behind as I followed the creek bed. The last people I saw were a pair of old ladies washing clothes in a fast little water channel. They seemed surprised when I stopped and said hello, their stony faces and hard eyes warming suddenly as they smiled and nodded shyly.

Then there was nothing but me and the mountains.

I had to choose between a grey-green bouldered valley on

my right and a red, snaggle-toothed rock formation on my left. I stood, shading my eyes with my hand, and surveyed the land.

Fate, in the form of a pack of feral dogs, decided my path for me. Out of a stand of thorny brush to my right came the first baying outriders. They crouched low and snarled at me, their white teeth bared, their lips curled. Then the rest of the pack made a flanking manoeuvre behind me, barking and snarling. The closest dogs, emboldened by reinforcements, began to inch closer, barking viciously, their hackles standing upright on their mangy backs. I've met a few packs of feral dogs in my life, but none so bent on my undoing as this lot were.

I stood tall and thanked myself for cutting a good stick and went for the closest dog. The light, green bamboo whistled through the air and missed his spittled jaws by a whisker. The others shrank back, barking louder and fiercer. I crouched slowly and picked up two fist-sized stones, my eyes on the closest, most dangerous-looking dogs. They shrank back even further because they knew what I was doing and I threw one of the stones hard at the ground in front of them. They yelped and sprang back and I walked slowly backwards towards the red rocks and the canyon. The dogs surged forward but I winged another rock at them; the dusty, red earth spat up in their faces and they cowered again. I carried on backing away and this time they didn't follow. My heart beat fast, I could hear the loud thump of adrenaline-gorged arteries in my ears and I was sweating hard. Then with excited, wobbly knees I wandered on.

I sit now with my back to the two foot thick wall of red rock which stretches thirty feet above me into the pale blue sky. The only sounds, apart from my own watery gulpings and the rattle of gravel beneath my feet, are of bees buzzing lazily past and the occasional tweet of a finch in the tall cacti below me.

All around are strange, absurdly coloured rock formations. It is dry, very dry. All the plants here are heavily armoured to protect their precious moisture – the shrubs are like thorny nests of barbed wire. The cacti, fifteen, twenty feet high and waxy green, are covered in three inch spines like hypo needles.

I would stay longer and draw it all but there's a canyon and a mountain behind me and a spliff in my pocket reserved for higher ground...

... puff... puff... ahhh...

I'm high above the valley floor now, spliff popping and smoking merrily in my hand, warm rock against my back.

The dry stream bed I followed wound up through the orange glow of the canyon, horse tracks on the sandy ground and scuttling lizards on the red rocks. I followed the trail steadily upwards for a while, wetting my hat in an ancient watering trough, until I came to a dry, boulder strewn valley which fell steeply into the cool of the canyon. Then I clambered up and up, white topped pampas grass, sweet wild herbs and football-sized cacti all around me.

I relished my solitude, singing as I climbed and climbing what I liked with delicious disregard for danger. Onto rock ledges I hauled myself and lay and panted and 'fuck – Icantbelieveljustdidthat' and kept an eye out for snakes and laughed and rose and climbed on. Then I came to the base of a sheer cliff, which must be an amazing waterfall with the rains, dry now. I couldn't climb it and the steep banks were pea-gravelled and sheer and I couldn't climb them either. So I stopped, and sat, and here I sit still. A quarter inch of spliff left and the rock still warm at my back.

The bands of colour which make up the valley below and the mountains beyond are so oddly contrasted that they look almost like an optical illusion. The white and green of the opposite slopes punctuated sharply by the canyons of red and orange, the shadows black and sharp. Then the grey-green dust of the valley floor, the little white houses of Tupiza and green eucalyptus trees by the railway. Then the whole scheme repeats itself in the glow and shadow of the canyon below me and the green of the scrub and the white gravel slopes in the foreground. Behind and above me, in the constant blue of the sky, two vultures soar. Now and then they swoop down through the canyon, legs dangling, ungainly below their majestic wings, the sunlight reflected off the rock beneath them colouring their bellies and the bulge of their wings. The birds are so big and the air is so quiet I can hear the loud whistling of the wind in their feathers from where I sit. I never associated flying with so much noise. It's always so quiet in my dreams...

... I'm sitting in the courtyard of a posada on the edge of town. Its crooked walls squat around what looks like a weeping willow tree. I lean back in my plastic chair and watch an old Alsatian bitch lying spreadeagled on the concrete. A motley crew of mongrels pad slowly round her, their tails down, sniffing her arse.

On the way back into town I saw a dog drink another dog's piss by the railway track. I've never seen that before. That is how dry this country is.

It is so dusty I can taste it on my lips as I take the first sip of my beer, earthy and good, condensation misting the green glass, cool in my hand. The other customers in the courtyard eyed me warily as I entered. There can't be a lot of gringos about considering the surprised and curious response of the locals at seeing a dusty Welshman with a stick of bamboo walk into a place like this. I don't mind their reaction. I'm still relishing my time as a solitary man.

I take another swig of beer and sigh contentedly and play with the handle of my stick. It is a fine stick, just the right length and weight. On my way back, leaping from boulder to boulder down the dry stream, it was a samurai sword. It became less and less so as I followed the railway back into town. Now it's just a walking stick again.

The sun must be setting now because the cliffs to my right are glowing a warm purple, casting soft light across the courtyard and this antiquated crew of drinkers. Plastic chairs and baseball caps are the only clue to what century it is and I feel happily adrift from reality again. But it's different from that snarled feeling of weightlessness I felt in La Paz. This is a kinder, more wholesome feeling. This is a drifting brought on by adrenaline and solitude, by hard play and a cold beer, by the timelessness of these people and this crooked old building and by the warm purple glow of the sunset on the red rock.

> Wander by, you dusty miners,
> your blackened faces and blackened clothes.
> Wander by, you ancient teenage mothers,
> your shawl-wrapped babies, young backs bowed.
> Wander by, you gnarled and sunburnt farmers,
> your skinny sheep and knock-kneed mule.
> Wander by and let this dusty paleface be,
> in the warm light of the mountain's glow.

Part Three

Part Three

20: Salta

If Peru was like an unwelcome guest, Bolivia was like a one-night stand. We kiss goodbye on the doorstep, happy to be leaving but polite enough not to let it show, not to be too rude. And while Bolivia wanders off to get a morning-after pill we sheepishly cross the border into the caring arms of Argentina, and she cries for us and we cry along with her. They are silent tears though, private tears, tears we no longer want to share. Lucy's gooseberry status has over-ripened on the bough, and for now not even the magpies of our old friendship will touch it. Mandy and I, as if we'd been unhappily married for years, keep up the self-conscious routine of love and companionship. But it is hollow, now that an end is in sight.

As our relationships change, the land through which we pass changes too. We come down from the high places and the air grows thick with oxygen. In the Andes we spent so much time talking about what it would be like to have enough air to breathe, but when we finally get it we forget in an instant what it felt like to choke for every breath, to struggle in lung and body.

As we move from the winter of the mountains to the late summer of Argentina we grow restless and short tempered, and in that mode we roll into the town of Salta at midnight, only to find that there is not enough room in our cleverly pre-booked inn. Room for one, but not for three. So Lucy stays and Mandy and I cross the street to another hostel and in our bunk we make sad, familiar love and the road and a chasm cuts us off from Lucy.

It is late morning by the time I wake up; the makeshift curtains we'd put up in the night were so effective that I slept until I could sleep no more. I feel refreshed and new, a feeling of spring is in me and I'm happy. I sit on the edge of the bed in my pants and watch Mandy sleep. She looks so peaceful and content, twitching now and then and snoring softly. A twinge of guilt hits me just below the ribs and I realise that I am pushing her away, that it is me that is ending this, not us.

I am doing what I have done so many times before, I think, watching her breasts rise and fall, her warm, smooth neck. *I met her and needed her, I broke down her defences with love and attention and I crawled inside. I idolised her and glamorised the new thing that our joining had created and it made me strong and happy. Then, when I was comfortable and secure, I began to see her faults and to judge her on them. Slowly I began to realise that she was not perfect, and ours was not a garden of love but a nest and a quiet place on a high and dusty road. I realised too that the nest we'd built was only temporary and the garden we'd visualised mocked us with its unobtainable beauty, its unrealistic expectations.*

But I wasn't being manipulative or calculating on purpose, I think. *What I felt was true and only looks cold and emotionless in retrospect. It is natural for a man and a woman to meet in lonely times and huddle together for safety and call it love. It is natural for that love to slowly fade and it is natural to walk away when it does.*

But the guilt is in my guts and it hurts, and I know it hurts because I am responsible for hurting Mandy. I sigh and rub my eyes with the palms of my hands, my elbows resting on my knees, and I turn and lean over her and kiss her on the sleeping lips. Sorry is waiting just inside my mouth, but I don't say it because I know it'd sound hollow and dry. Instead I get up, grab a towel and slip out of the door.

Sometimes guilt or sadness can follow me for days. Sometimes I almost relish misery and sweet melancholia. But not today. Today the sky is blue and the sun is warm and there is a smell in the air of roots and trees and rich, dark earth and as I close the door to the room I cut the twisted strings of self pity and regret and they fall away behind me, and I am happy again.

By the light of day our hostel is even prettier than it had been at midnight. It is a sprawling one-storey townhouse of whitewashed plaster and rusty roof tiles. In the high-walled courtyard a little fountain tinkles and the sounds of the road outside are muffled by a mess of climbing roses and Virginia creeper. I smile to myself and almost skip along the cool hall to the bathroom.

Clean and dry I walk into the little kitchen where a group of backpackers are playing cards at a table. They are clean and healthy-looking and I feel hunched and tired compared to them, as if the high country and tough travel have sucked something out of me that they have in spades. I feel tough though, a swarthy cowboy in clean, polite society with a thousand-mile-stare and a fresh scar. I relish the way they look at me and look away and I quietly make a coffee and sit down next to them and wait until I've lit a cigarette before smiling and saying hello.

I like them already, this lot. They're not the soppy English gap-year 'doers', or the overenthusiastic, once-in-a-lifetime 'must-see-ers'. Just a pleasant group of people from all over the place who happened to come together for a game of cards one day, and I just happened to pull up a chair and join in.

Three of them are Aussies: Matty, Beth and Amy. One of them is American: Aaron. And now one of them is Welsh: Uncle Willy.

We play President and laugh and it's good to meet new people, good to have no painful strings attached to me, good to have a clean slate. I soon come down off my high, cowboy horse, and my thousand-mile-stare becomes a smiling twinkle. I feel like I'm back on track and that fate has chosen me a new path.

They are going camping in a couple of hours, they tell me, next to a lake in the hills. I invite myself along and, after a little twinge of conscience, I invite my sleeping girlfriend along too and they smile and agree, and in that great, self-sufficient Aussie way they tell me to get the hell on with it or they'll leave without me.

So I wake up Mandy with hot coffee and forced gaiety and tell her about my new friends and the camping trip. I can tell she feels that spring-like hope in the air too and she's happy and when I leave the room to get money and supplies those twisted strings have left us both and the end has again been postponed.

Salta is a shock to the system. I'm so accustomed to dry, dusty towns and everyday harshness that it seems like we've gone through a secret door into an alternate reality, a reality in which Europe has been moved to South America, and is happily shading itself among the long, leafy boulevards and the elegant old buildings.

I hurry through the clean streets and wonder at all the

different colours of the people. No one looks at me, no one notices that I'm a gringo, no one hassles me. I am one of many white faces in a sea of different colours. I am no longer taller than everyone else, I'm no longer a walking dollar sign, and my halo of first-world guilt and unfairness has dimmed to the faintest of auras.

As I wait in line to use the shiny cash machine, next to a crisp, white nurse and a pinstriped businessman, I suddenly feel very scruffy in my dirty old trainers and grubby clothes. I feel inelegant and ungainly for the first time in months and shockingly it makes me feel at home. And I smile. I smile because I know that for now the hard bit is done. I smile because I know that leg-breaking bus seats and sour-milk Cholos are a thing of the past, because I have survived and because I have grown.

Back at the hostel Mandy is waiting and happy and the others have gone on ahead to the bus station. I throw everything I don't need into bin-liners, put them in a cupboard, and with light rucksacks and a clinking bag of booze we hail a cab with a meter and join the others.

They're sitting on their rucksacks with a couple of Israeli lads, surrounded by plastic bags full of food and bottles. Mandy and I are introduced and we sit down too. They're waiting for another ten Israelis. In all there will be nineteen of us going camping. A large and safe posse, a crew where once there was just a few.

Talk is of camping and drinking and the lake as we wait for the bus, in Hebrew and Aussie, Yank and Manc. I still feel like it's all not quite real. Everything is so familiarly western, the roads are swept and well metalled, the petrol stations clean and shiny, the cars slick and modern. There is no ingrained grime, no old women selling popped corn and sugared nuts, yelling and yodelling the song of their wares.

There are no mules, no cacti and, most noticeably, no dust. The strangest thing is that I'm not sure which reality is more unreal – the present or the past few months.

The bus we ride and the roads down which it drives are entirely normal. There is no sullen co-driver in a rotten pullover to take the fares, and no small boys get on to sell sweets or schoolbooks. There are no wonders of human endurance, no lean-tos of corrugated iron and burlap, no dog packs or swaggering soldiers. I feel at once glad to be home and sad that the time of simplicity and safety in foreignness and shared danger is over.

I sit and brood and watch the world flash by outside my fly-streaked window. It is poplars and suburbs, the world. It is football fields and schools. It is churches and car-lots. It is harmonious. It is easy. It holds no extremes and no imminent, unavoidable danger. Then it's the country and when it's the country I relax and my brooding leaves me and I pop the cap off a beer and the few passengers who aren't coming camping with us shake their head with pious disapproval as we pass it around.

In a packed-dirt yard beside the road we sit on our packs. The bus from Salta dropped us off here and the driver told us that another bus will come along at some unspecified time to take us the rest of the way. The Aussies and Yanks sit together on one side, the Israelis on the other. The Manc wanders about the yard spooking scrawny hens and kicking pebbles and I, free to once again be a people-person now that I have people to be a person with, wander between the groups finding out who's who and what's what.

All of the Israelis have been recently discharged from the army. Those who were of higher rank still have a certain detachment from the others, a noticeable superiority. We pass a bottle of rum between us and I tell them about my travels so far and they tell me about theirs. The girls are pretty and dark and the guys are tall, well built and confident. I can't help feeling there's a guardedness in them though, an expectation just below the surface that I might suddenly start berating them for what Israel is doing to Palestine, and this makes them defensive even though I haven't mentioned politics at all.

Well maybe I've mentioned Chavez once or twice.

And maybe my eyes did shine with a righteous, left-wing lustre...

Soon though we're chatting excitedly, soon the rum kicks in, soon the groups mix and we're looking around for some means of getting to the lake and our camping grounds because the bus is taking its sweet time and the party is getting restless.

And soon too the next bus comes and the driver's eyes are surprised to see so many well-stocked foreigners in the middle of nowhere. We pile on and our spirits are high from the rum. We talk loudly and laugh and the woods through which we drive flash by our windows, the sun dapples the road and the spring feeling in me is stronger, and I can't help but smile.

The bus leaves us in a little village and we descend en masse upon the village shop and buy more cold beers and ice creams and ask directions to the lake. The old woman behind the counter and her dark-eyed nephew bustle about in happy, flustered sorties to the stock room and back and soon we've bought more than we can carry.

They tell us that the lake is five miles away and that we'd better watch out for the local boys because they can be rough sometimes. I look about at our Israeli guard and try to imagine a pack of lads strong or crazy enough to play rough with this lot and I smile and thank them and wonder if there are any locals with a pick-up who might help us out. The old lady says that her son might fancy a little extra income, so her nephew leads Aaron the Yank and a couple of the Israelis down a side street to a house with firewood stacked high against its gable end. They knock on the door to beg a ride while the rest of us sit on the curb and devour our ice creams and pass the rum around.

Soon we've split into two groups and then I'm sitting on a mound of packs in the back of an old, red pick-up and the warm wind whistles in my ears and I light a ciggie and it burns fast and one-sided and I grin at the woods and the warmth and I catch myself and I laugh.

Beside the wide and wind-moved lake we pull up and run from clearing to clearing, trying to find a spot suitable for a large and drunken crew of campers, and the driver shakes his wide, brown head and tells us we'll find nowhere here and we ask him why he brought us here and he shrugs and we climb back on top a little bemused and fly off again towards an old campsite on the far shore.

The evening is setting in now and the clouds to the east are purple and we still haven't found a place to camp. The other group are still waiting by the shop and we turn off the road where an old and tattered sign advertises camping spaces with barbeques. The iron mesh gates are closed and the track looks unused and the grass in the fields is knee high and dusty horses crop and swish their tails. It looks deserted but we have no other option so we squeeze between the gates and jog down the track towards a little wooden house on the shore. Two scrawny dogs come leaping and baying out to meet us and I hang back but the Israeli with me keeps his pace and the dogs wag their tails and keep their distance.

We jog up to the house and knock on the battered old door. After a while a crusty old man opens it suspiciously, looking like a hermit with his grimy smock and matted hair. We chatter excitedly that we are the outriders of a great party needing shelter and barbeque pits for the night and he grumbles and whines and snags a chain of keys from a hook with a hook-like hand and stalks off to open the gates.

Then we're piling packs in the long grass and the little red truck has gone to pick up the others and I wade towards the barbeque pits with grasshoppers leaping ahead of me like dolphins. The air is thick with summer smells, the only sounds are the horses ripping and chomping grass and the bees buzzing overhead.

By now the west is pink and the east is dark purple and we have neither firewood nor tents pitched. So I shake the peace and lullaby sleepiness of the meadow from my head and climb a dead apple tree and dismantle it from the top down and I yell to the Israeli lads cavorting like a pair of spring lambs to do the same and soon we have a mound of wood and spiders and soon too the others have chugged up and are leaping and gambolling in the meadow and for a moment in the dusky golden light everything is beautiful.

Then it's gone and instead it's activity and tents and I'm surprised at how lame and lost these fine army types are until they're issued orders.

Soon it's dark and the leaping flames rip and snap at the stars and Mandy and I sit down together for the first time since I sat with her this morning. I am lost between the beauty and the peace that lingers in my soul and the numb guilt which hovers just below the surface. I lean over and hug her and we feel warm and good and the others can see how happy we are, but it's not true and we both know it. She says something mildly cutting and I snap defensively. We're still holding on to each other, but it's a cold and forced cling now and the others can see that too.

So I sigh and rise and, wanting to be jolly, I head for the Aussies where they're cooking and laughing and drinking rum. Matty the Aussie reminds me of a couple of my favourite friends in his humour and respectful banter and soon we're pissed as a pair of old winos and laughing fit to burst. Now and then I covertly look over at Mandy and she's laughing too and covertly looking over at me and I try to turn resentment into acceptance, but I'm terrible at it so I accept my resentment instead and that makes me feel okay, odd but okay.

The night goes on like this: we drink and laugh, we play stupid drinking games thrust upon us by the drunken Aussie girls. We climb trees for firewood and fun. We smoke weed in the long grass with an Israeli hip-hopper, an American twang to his guttural accent. Mandy and I go for a walk by the lake because both of us are horny, but there's too much resentment and drunken stumbling in our words to get us together. So instead of finding a good spot to roll around we wander aimlessly about instead.

Bored and frustrated when we're together, horny and happy when we're apart. It's no way to live, no way at all.

As I get more drunk, I get more horny and the Israeli girls get more attractive. I laugh with them but I know that Mandy can see me, and I know that I don't have it in me to be that much of a bastard. So I laugh and smile, but I hurt inside from all the effort and guilt and horniness and booze. And that soup of emotion inside me eventually sends me to bed.

It's nearly light and I lie there drunk and restless until Mandy stumbles in. We don't say anything and that affords us enough leeway to snuggle and sleep in each other's arms.

I wake up sticky and sweaty in the airless tent with the midday sun beating the crap out of my aching head through the dark nylon. Mandy is sweating and snoring beside me and my throat and mouth are thick with dehydration. I groan and grumble and fiddle claustrophobically with the zip until I get it open and breathe a lungful of fresh air. The sleepy meadow has turned into a landfill site – one of the horses is munching on a crusty stick of French bread and the old man's billy goat is dragging its tether and haughtily sniffing at the bodies of a couple of Israelis, sleeping where they fell.

I groan again and search for my sunglasses to block the sun's assault. Then I search for water and find only beer and it's warm but I pop the cap anyway and guzzle half a litre before stopping to breathe and belch.

I wander about, half-heartedly picking up rubbish and sloshing back beers until I'm drunk again and the pain in my head has reduced enough for me to concentrate on the sweaty discomfort of my clothes and sticky crust of my eyes. Soon others join me and we mill about like zombies and eventually corral the vicious billy and tether him again. We take photos of his prestigious nut sack and that lightens our mood and we're laughing again and drunk again and so crusty that we have to swim, like it or not.

The lake is so still it's like diving into glass. Until I break the surface and suddenly everything is cold and dark and quiet. The sun is all I can see, high up through the peat-brown water. The air I brought down with me rushes past, tickling as it goes and flashing in the sunlight. I wait and watch it go, and then I follow until I pop out again, into a bubble of colour and sound, and a feeling of health and cold cleanliness and a realisation that I'm drunk in the morning and I can breathe and the sun is warm, even if the lake is cold enough to turn my balls to walnuts. Spontaneously we laugh at the water and at each other. We splash about and then Mandy is squatting by the water and I smile at her too, but it's not a spontaneous smile. Again I'm doing maths with my emotions and it all equals out as resentment and numbness.

I dive again and this time I stay down longer. I imagine that all the confused blackness in my guts is flowing out of me like tar, sinking to the black bottom, to interlock with years of silt and death. When I kick up towards the sun I try to leave it all behind and below me. I try to escape it, but when I break the surface she's still sitting on the bank, looking hangdog and glum, and the guilt and defensiveness is still mine, still mine.

Back in Salta I can feel the change in me stronger than ever. Just getting my stuff out of the cupboard and seeing the dusty old weariness of it all makes me realise that I am different already. In two days I have adapted so much that it's hard to imagine how I felt in Bolivia, how it felt to be breathless and half desperate all the time. I have learnt and grown and callously moved on, shedding Mandy and Lucy like a snakeskin. I feel guilty, yet somehow I feel that I didn't knowingly do anything wrong. I was just me being me and I did what I do, none of it was out of character. I don't know if that's reassuring or scary...

21: Cordoba (crouching crackhead, hidden junkie)

The last time I saw Lucy her feet were filthy from night after night of partying in flip-flops. That's what they call Laurel and Hardy in Poland – Flip i Flop. My Polish friends couldn't understand why I thought it was funny. They couldn't understand why I insisted on calling them Laurel and Hardy.

Lucy couldn't understand my silent concern, my conviction that she was going too hard, too far, too fast. When I saw Lucy in a restaurant in Salta, she, like us, had a new crew. We trooped in for famous Argie steaks a few days after the lake,

Aussies and Yanks, but no Israelis, and found her and her crew already tucking in. She had an Aussie. Her Aussie was smoking an ornately carved pipe and discussing wine with the waiter. She had cockneys too, ones she'd met when she was in Colombia. We sat in an adjacent booth. We had no cockneys and our Aussies had no pipes, but I like it better that way. We were good and polite and old friends again.

'This is Willy,' she said to her crew. They nodded, they'd heard about me, they smiled warmly.

'This is Lucy,' I said to my crew. They smiled warmly, they'd heard about her, they nodded.

And that was pretty much that. We'd obviously made an unspoken decision to travel separately, to go the same way and meet occasionally along the road but to go separately, and I liked it that way too.

The steaks were fine, so was the wine, and oh how civilised we all felt, oh how noble. Though we all agreed that the pipe was a little excessive, in one so young.

We didn't know then that he was mad, Lucy's Aussie, and flying high circles on anti-psychotics and elephant tranqs, but Lucy knew and she'd accepted him, and the cockneys too, so I did the same.

Those days were odd, like some days are. The transition between the high places and low took a long time to sink in. The buses were clean and flash and what went on tour stayed on tour, forgotten by morning in a haze of downers and fine wines.

It was odd too that Mandy and I took so long to go our separate ways, damaging each other in our reluctance to break habit. Speaking seldom and fighting when we did. Fucking only occasionally and with a vicious, sadistic energy. Making hate, making confusion, making numbness.

When I hide from myself, and beat about the emotional bush, I become a bad drunk. Not violent, but almost. Not aggressive, but not nice either. I became a muttering, shaded drunk. My new friends, Aussies and Yank alike, don't really know me as anything else, though on sullen, hungover mornings I try to explain that I'm not usually like this, I'm usually a pretty chilled guy, really I am. Mandy and guilt and normality twisting me out of shape, bending my sanity off the ground and skywards, as we travelled southwards, winterwards and down.

Down, one day, to Cordoba. Cordoba hunched like Birmingham in a maze of industry and noise, concrete and bums. Off a bus one grey drizzling dawn and out into the slimy streets.

I still have my bamboo samurai walking stick and dust tattooed into my trainers. I still have Mandy and my new crew and I still have my backpack. Cordoba, at this time of day, doesn't care.

We navigate through the city blocks, alone apart from yappy dogs walking their old men and huddled bums like overcoat ghosts, alone apart from night shift cabbies and early shift grafters.

We find the street we're trying to find and it's an alarming tribute to human shit and dog shit and pigeon shit all musty and some steaming and all odorous and we trudge down it, our spirits heading the same way, and we grin grim grins and tough it out until we reach the place we're trying to reach. A hostel, that place, with a little café in the front, condensation windows and damp people, cats in the courtyard and an old bike rigged to sharpen knives. A hostel unfriendly enough to make the meanest parasite feel unwelcome. We are too tired to care. We drank too much on the way here to care. We heard from people coming north as we headed south that this was the place to be, but now we're here we're just too damn tired to be disappointed.

So we sleep until midday in a room big enough to hold all six of us, Welsh Wil, Manc Mandy, Yank Aaron and Aussies Matty, Beth and Amy, all sleeping and snoring and muttering and farting in an old room, high-ceilinged and temporary.

When we get up it's still raining, and just as gloomy as six in the morning. It looks like London; that underwater feeling of diffused sunlight and filmy wetness that sucks the colour from the world and weighs like shitbales on my soul.

I can't face it. I pretend to sleep as the others tiptoe around me and I concentrate on making my breathing low and slow, and keeping my eyelids from flickering while they discuss whether or not they should wake me so I can come to the cinema too. I almost laugh when Mandy says, 'Let's just fooking leave him,' with distaste in her tone.

I stay pretending to sleep long enough to be safe that no one has forgotten anything and no one will come back. Then I turn on the TV and flick channels looking for something vaguely pornographic to watch. I eventually find a swimwear catwalk show on the fashion channel and masturbate; an idea that models are like racehorses or giraffes pops into my mind as I come and when I come I feel even more colourless and grey. I mop up in the bathroom and avoid my reflection in the mirror, not from masturbatory guilt, but because I'm scared that my reflection will be colourless, grey and filmy too.

I flop back on the bed and my appreciation for racehorses in skimpy knickers is zero and my appreciation of Cordoba is less. I know I have to get out of the room or I'll become irreparably negative and cease to exist at all.

Outside I huddle into my hoodie and stomp through the streets almost relishing the light drizzle and the wet brick and exhaust smells because they remind me of London and they make me happily homesick and melancholy.

I have an idea that smoking weed will save my soul today

and so I wander for blocks looking for the grimiest poolhalls and dodgiest bars but it's too early in the day and it's too damp and miserable so I duck into a shitty little restaurant and order a beer and then sit back and wonder why the fuck I ducked into this place. The TV on the wall is blaring fast Latin American football commentary, screaming now and then 'GOOOOOOOOOOOOOOOOOOOOOOOOOOOOOOOOAL!' The jukebox is loud and screaming constant synthetic salsa-waltzes and the bums at the bar and the football fans at the tables have to shout to make themselves heard, even those who are alone and talking to themselves.

I am alone but I'm not talking to myself. I'm smoking endless cigarettes and drinking glasses of ice-cold beer from a huge bottle the dumpy waitress brought me. She has black roots under her curly peroxide mop, like a bad case of dry rot.

I'm not hungry but I know I have to eat so I order watery ravioli and poke it around the plate while my cigarette burns in the ashtray and the smoke of the bar stings my tired eyes.

I sit there and finish as much of the food as is reasonable and I finish my beer and order another. I try not to look at the TV or the steaming drunks at the bar or the soggy waitress. I try not to look out the window because the world is a fish tank today and there is precious little joy anywhere; the fish are dead, oxygen starved and floating on the surface. I think of Brautigan and his dead fish and cum story and I find a little joy in *Trout Fishing in America*, but it's temporary, a fleeting half-remembered joy which doesn't last long.

After a while I spy the others trudging, avoiding puddles, up the road and I wonder whether I should pretend to be asleep again, but I'm lonely and I walk to the door, leaving my cap on the table so the frumpy waitress won't worry that I'm leaving without paying the bill.

The others see me leaning by the door there and their faces

tell me that they know the fish are dead too and they wander in behind me. All the bums at the bar and the football fans look up and see the girls as they enter and suddenly I know they shouldn't be in here. I try to ignore their leering and leaning-in and we make a diversionary fuss putting tables together and ordering beers. I halve the order in translation so we'll drink quicker and give the bums and leering football fans less time to make their seedy play at the girls. Aaron the Yank looks uncomfortable and Matty the Aussie looks quietly amused. The girls are oblivious.

They tell me they've been to the cinema, because I was clever enough to ask them where they've been, and they didn't enjoy the movie, and they haven't seen any joy either. I start telling them about Brautigan's cum and dead fish story but it's useless and too personal, and anyway the most drunk of the bums has decided to make his play before the others can get it together.

In filthy slacks he lurches up and starts pawing at Mandy with his eyes and frowsy rum-breath, and because tact has gone the way of joy and colour, I tell him politely to go fuck his mother. He baulks and mutters but turns his attention once again to Mandy. I can feel that I have no patience and he's scraping at the thin layer of humility I have left and soon there will be none at all. I look desperately towards the squinting waitress and she nods from behind the bar and comes to our table and tells the bum to cool it. She knows his name and calls him it but he still pays her no mind. Mandy tells him to fook off but her Spanish is bad and he lays his grubby-nailed paw on her leg and leans in closer. I stand up quickly and everyone else tenses, but mercifully the waitress steps in between us, grabs his collar and marches him to the door like a naughty schoolboy. I smile and nod gratefully at her while the bum stands in the doorway telling me about my mother and saying he'll be waiting for me and I smile and nod and wave back. The football fans and bar-bums tut and look away in half-hearted disgust. I feel like a dead fish myself now.

'I could have handled that myself,' Mandy says to me when we've calmed down a bit.

'I couldn't,' I tell her and we laugh nervously and finish our self-conscious beers and pay and thank the glowing waitress and wander out into the rain.

Back in the room the bottoms of our trousers are damp and there's a musty smell of wet shit coming from our shoes and we sit about on the beds and dejectedly wonder what the fuck brought us to Cordoba in the first place.

'This is shit,' says someone.

'True,' says someone else.

And it is true, it is shit.

'Let's just leave,' says someone.

'Let's,' says everyone else.

Why we hadn't thought of it before I don't know. I suppose some sense of politeness or a need to 'give it a chance' held us back, like we owed Cordoba something, like we were obliged to stay. Not any more.

Suddenly there is joy and everyone is smiling and packing and wondering how much we should pay for our half-day room.

Then, just as we think it's safe to escape, two men put their heads in at the door. They're both grinning with naughty broken teeth and polyester sports clothing. One of them has no ears.

'Aarait?' says the one with no ears in a Scouse accent.

'Ellow,' says the other, peering over his friend's shoulder.

'Hey,' I say, nearest to the door and them. 'Hey,' like I don't want to talk to them. 'Hey,' like I'd rather not have another dead fish bobbing so close to my side of the tank. 'Hey,' like 'go away'. They don't care.

'When did you guys get in?' asks No-Ears with adenoidal enthusiasm.

'This morning,' I say. The others stop packing and watch wearily.

'Oh yeah?' says Ears. 'You're not leavin now are ye? Dis place is fookin greit.'

He doesn't care that we don't care, neither of them do.

'Yeah,' says No-Ears, 'we've got these crazy crack-whores livin in the next room and one of them's got this crazy kid and dey sell us kewk and sook our nobs.'

'Yeah. It's fookin sound,' says Ears. 'D'you wanna buy an iPod?'

I want to cry. The bastards have stolen my last slice of humility and now all I have left is gritted teeth and a will to survive.

'No thanks, lads,' I say, straightening up from my packing, summoning my reserves. 'You don't have any weed do you?' I ask.

'Where're you from?' asks No-Ears, ignoring my question.

'North Wales,' gritting my teeth for the inevitable:

'Har-har fookin sheep shagger,' says Ears.

'Fuck you, scally twat,' I grumble good naturedly, my eyes dying from the injustice of it all.

Apart from Mandy none of our crew have ever been this close to scallies before, they don't know what to make of them. They hang back and smile disconcertedly, unable to work out the meaning of this constant abuse and the ever shifting eyes. It's like watching a baby mongoose meet a cobra for the first time – it knows it doesn't like the slimy, evil creature in front of it but it isn't sure why. Better kill it just in case.

'You don't have any weed then?' I ask again.

'No, la,' they say together.

'I've got some Valiums though, blueys,' says No-Ears.

'How much?' I ask.

'How much do you wanna pay?' asks Ears, like it's a big fucking joke, grinning like a cock.

'Nothing,' I snap, losing patience again. 'Fucking nothing, shit-for-brains.'

Then: 'Sorry lads,' getting a hold of myself. 'I've had a bit of a morning of it. Give us five for a peso. How's that sound?'

'Fook off!' says No-Ears, sitting down on my bed, pulling out a plastic pill bottle. 'Five for two pesos,' he says.

'Ten for two fifty,' I say. The mongooses are watching me now, looking at me like I might be a scally too, like I might be slimy and evil, but there's admiration there too. I give them a conspiratorial wink.

'Alright,' says No-Ears to me, fumbling with the bottle cap.

'Alright?' says Ears to Mandy, smiling ingratiatingly.

'Yeh,' says Mandy to Ears, returning his smile.

'I'll take twenty,' I say to No-Ears and he counts them out onto his skinny, pink palm.

'Where you from?' Ears asks Mandy.

'Manchester,' Mandy tells Ears.

'There you go,' I hand No-Ears the fiver.

'Cheers,' he says.

'Whereabouts in Manchester?' Asks Ears.

'Right,' I say, cutting across their budding conversation, putting the pills in my pocket and patting them safe, 'are we ready?'

'Yes,' the Aussies and the Yank say together, a little too enthusiastically.

We pick up our packs and start towards the door, shepherding the Scousers out in front of us. Outside it's still raining and the crack-whores are coming across the courtyard towards us. There are three of them and a vicious-looking boy of about seven. They all look as mean as rubbish-dump rats.

'Hello sexy,' says No-Ears to the one with no teeth.

'¿Que?' she asks, spitting a lungful into the gutter.

'Okay. Nice one guys,' I say loudly, smiling through gritted teeth and grabbing dawdling Mandy by the hand and half-dragging her towards the street. The others are ahead of us already paying and handing in the key.

'You should stay, Welshy,' Ears calls after me. 'This place is fookin greit!'

I don't have an answer. I'm not even a dead fish any more, they've taken that from me too, I'm just fish skin now, Lieutenant W. Fishskin, and I want to go home.

But that isn't all, that isn't all at all.

In the bus terminal we hole up under strip lights in a café with Formica tables and screechy metal chairs. We order beers and make sandwiches and play poker with coins and then notes. The staff watch us worriedly, but a little impressed too, as we drink fast and laugh loud and dig in for the three hour wait for the bus to Mendoza.

In two hours we are loud and pissed and reckless. Aaron the Yank is a pale shade of green because of the shellfish he'd had for lunch and the beers he'd had for dinner. He lurches up and stumbles towards the toilets but doesn't make it and pukes a loud ralphing puke into a rubbish bin. Passers-by pass by pretending not to notice, looks of disgust or mild amusement on their faces.

The café staff are not amused, they're looking worried now. Aaron sits back down and belches, his big, friendly head still green and bloodless. We congratulate him noisily and he half manages a smile. We are becoming animals now. Life is a farmyard and we are the pigs.

But maybe the farmyard makes pigs what they are. Maybe if Cordoba hadn't treated us to so many bums and Scousers we wouldn't be behaving like animals ourselves. Maybe...

'What's the bet I can't get this in that rubbish bin over there?' I ask Matty, balling a piece of paper in my hands.

'Never,' says Matty with a slight slur.

'Just fucking watch me,' I say, also with a slight slur.

I wing the ball of paper high and long and it looks good but when it's at the highest point of its trajectory the terminal door opens and through it steps a fine, upstanding Naval officer in full dress uniform. Purposefully he marches right into the line of fire and the paper ball catches him smartly on the back of the head. He spins round and look – there's a crew of drunk gringos with their table piled high with empties and half-empties and overflowing ashtrays and pistachio shells and cards and money. They're all looking this way. I wonder who could have thrown that ball of paper.

'So like I was saying,' I say quickly, loudly, as if I was interrupted mid-flow by an angry Naval officer, 'if the farmer loved his pigs and God loved us sheep, what need would there be for shepherds, sheep, pigs or farmers at all? What need have we for God? After all we're just dead fish floating in a stream of cum and dark water.'

And the Naval officer turns smartly on his heels and the staff of the café and the passers-by turn away and shake their heads with disappointment and half-hearted disgust, and I lay my head down on the table and groan.

Can I go home yet? Please?

22: Mendoza

No. You can't go home yet. Not until you've done what you came out here to do.

What did I come out here to do?

I don't know.

Then how will I know when I've done it?

You'll know.

But how?

Stop asking so many dumb questions and relax!

It's fucking hard to relax when you're being so evasive.

I'm not being evasive. I merely mean to point out that you can accomplish nothing until you let go.

But if I don't know what I'm supposed to accomplish, and I don't know what I have to let go of, how can I hope to get anywhere?

You're already somewhere.

Where am I?

Mendoza.

So?

So you're somewhere.

But this still doesn't give me a good enough reason not to go home.

Have you thought that maybe you're being a bit wet?

What?

You're being wet. You're being a pussy.

No I'm not!

Yes you are. Take Mandy for instance. You should have dumped her ages ago.

Yeah, well...

You beat around the bush and fuck yourself up with booze and soft drugs and bad relationships, you accomplish nothing constructive and then you have the gall to feel sorry for yourself.

I have accomplished constructive things. I'm building a past for myself. When I look back on this time it'll be like reading Bukowski.

Bollocks.

"S'not bollocks.

Yes it is. Bukowski's a parasite.

But he writes well.

Yes but he's an arsehole. You're not even committed to being a whole arsehole. You're just an arsehole with a conscience: half an arsehole.

Okay. Now you're just being offensive.

You drive me to it. You're so self-important and egotistical, yet you accomplish nothing.

Here we go again. I do accomplish stuff. At least I will.

So get rid of Mandy then.

Okay.

Now.

Okay!

I'm in the bathroom, towel around my waist, talking to myself in the mirror. In my head.

I know what I have to do.

We arrived here this morning. Off another bus and into the dappled autumn sunshine of Mendoza. Orange and yellow leaf-lined streets, wide and stately. Fountains and dark, beautiful women. Acres of tangled vineyards on the outskirts of town, flashing optical illusions of parallel rows horizontal and diagonal from the speeding bus windows. Angry looking clowns at the traffic lights juggling for pennies.

It's disconcerting how you can travel from season to season as you travel from town to town. None of it makes any sense really; I go to sleep in spring and wake up in winter, sleep in winter and wake up in autumn. It makes predicting the future so much harder – forcing me into that Zen-like immediacy of being, that enforced state of nowness.

Now... where was I?

I'm in the bathroom, towel around my waist. Dimly trying to ignore the memories of Cordoba as they bob momentarily into my mind before slipping into the past. I know what I have to do. I have to split up with Mandy. For the good of all, not just for myself.

I dress with dread, eat breakfast with foreboding, and find Mandy and the others with resolution squishing and kneading at my heart. I am aware that there should be some joy in having finally made the decision to get rid of her. I can find none.

'Hey guys,' I say with pathetic chirpiness.

'Hey!'

'G'day!'

'Morning!'

'Hello mate!'

'Alright?' come the responses in chorus.

'Er... Mandy,' I say with a pathetic smile, 'd'you think I could have a word?'

'Yeah,' she says, getting up, exchanging a 'here we go' glance with Amy.

So here we go.

We descend the stairs into our empty dorm-room. She knows what I'm doing. I can smell her defensive righteousness.

'What?' she demands when we're both sitting on an unused bunk.

'Um,' I start.

Just get on with it!

'I think we should call it a day.'

'Call what a day?' She already knows.

'Us,' I reply.

'I thought we already had,' she says with smart-arse bitterness.

'Um...' I don't know what to say to that.

'Wil,' she starts. Here we go. 'You've been a right bastard to me y'know? Since we left Bolivia you've been really grumpy and rude. I don't know why I've stayed with you.'

'Really?' I'm lost in her logic already.

'Yeah,' she's picking up steam now, 'you were right nice to me in the beginning and then you started being weird and bad to me. I reckon you were just using me.'

'Oh.' I am Cannot Be Bothered. Sir Cannot Be Bothered of the East.

'Yeah, and I saw you chatting up that Israeli girl when we were camping. And that American girl. And that waitress. D'you think I'm stupid?'

Yes.

'No.' *Yes. Yes. Yes.* 'No. I don't think you're stupid, Mandy. Let's not be like this, eh? Let's try and make this as mature and reasonable as possible, eh? C'mon, you know I never set out to hurt you or use you. It just didn't work out is all.'

'Because of you,' bottom lip protruding, arms crossed. 'You're a fooking bastard.'

'Aw c'mon M,' abbreviating endearingly. 'You know I think the world of you.' I hug her rigid torso, stroke her tensed back muscles. Fucking duplicitous arsehole.

Ha! So I am an arsehole?

Fucking shady twat.

You told me to do it!

I didn't tell you to ditch her and then give her a patronising hug when she doesn't want one.

She does want one really. Look she's relaxing... There – she's even snotting on my shoulder.

Bastard. I thought I was supposed to be the bad cop.

We both are.

'Why did you ever ask me to come with you?' She's blubbing now. 'I knew I shouldn't have come.'

'Hey,' I say kindly, 'we had some fun didn't we? What about that night on Titicaca? That was fun.'

'That was shit,' she says and cries harder.

That *was* shit.

'Yeah,' I say dreamily, 'it was shit.'

'Look,' she says, realising that I'm being a bastard, pulling away from me. 'Why don't you just fook off?'

And she curls up with her back to me, her hair all crazy and frizzy, bouncing with every sob. I sit there feeling like shit. I am a bastard. I am an arsehole. Somehow this doesn't feel as good as I thought it would.

Did you think it was going to feel good?

I guess not. I guess I hoped it might though.

What are you going to do now?

I guess we've split up. I guess I'll go away. I guess I'm free.

Feels good doesn't it?

Yeah... yeah it does. And the light slowly beings to shine. The light of joy.

Bit bad about her though.

Yeah. Look at her there. I feel guilty.

Don't worry. She'll be okay. I bet this happens to her all the time.

Bastard.

Arsehole.

I love you Willy.

I love you too.

'I'm sorry M,' I say and I say it in a different voice to the one I was using before. There's nothing pleading or placating about this voice. This is my real voice:

'I'm sorry we stretched it out for so long. I'm sorry I turned off the love. I'm sorry it had to end like this.'

And I lean over and kiss her cheek and see that her eyes are open and there are tears on her cheeks and she's staring at the wall.

'Yeah,' she says bitterly, 'you were just using me.'

And I shrug and I sigh and know I handled it badly.

But at least it's done.

Part Four

23: Buenos Aires (the Millhouse)

Like a strangled lamb, my entrance upon this next stage seems like the first breath of life choked rattling-dry with the same fateful umbilical cord which brought me here, which fed me this, this Buenos Aires...

Enter the three of us. Enter I, the sheepishest of sheep unto this new fold, I who drowned in rum and was reborn a monster-for-the-night and woke again in crumpled sorry ovine form. I at whose eyes the magpie crushing sharp-cornered roar of the city pecks and tears and all my mind will say is: Run! Escape! Get Out!

I hear it not; only the coffee swirling sugar in molasses-black and foaming cup exists, only the throbbing thump of my blood, the clicking glue-stuck clack of my dry and swollen tongue. All else is false. All else can suffer without this strangled lamb.

In twisted form forth we herd away from the bus-fume froth, diesel black and sinus ache, playing follow-the-leader through crowds faceless, unseen by me, whose eyes are for the paves alone for fear of crying tears of sheepish blood and drowning in it all. All these fifteen million soulless souls encased in steel and girdered concrete stale, a heaving hive of termite mounds and wounds, each one as un-unique and pitiful-lost as the next; every one a marvel of inverted evolution, each subspecies clotting wax-cooled and coagulated until nothing remains but the whole, a hole much less the sum of its festered parts and no less heavy upon my tired back and knotted shoulders bent.

Get Out! Escape! My drumless march as best hoof forward on we trot, entangled, stuck in porno theatre and club foot beggar's piss, in vicious eyes not ten years old and blackened nail and tooth. Above shines disgust and hovers high as if it was the sun itself and below in darkness thick I walk, in treacle socks and tearstained footrot boots.

And then a door. A door within a door in fact, with fish eye circuit closed above and doorbell quiet expectant buzz and enter. And enter.

Enter windowless and striplit flicker glare: another world. Enter the backpack factory, the flat-pack bento thrill-seeking peek into a world devoid of worldliness, and in wordless horror stare as through this droning room of clones a ghost of realisation stalks:

That though we are many, we privileged few, it is not just I that am the ewe, but We.

All thoughts collide in league to flee, but not an inch my clogged pores move, so on their guestbook ledger goes, in twitching pen-clasped claw I scrawl, my number, my name and my country.

'And how long will you be staying with us?' asks, uniformed and un-spectacular, the deskside shepherdess in drawl.

I cannot answer. How do the damned answer the demon-clerk at gates of hell?

'For ever and ever, Amen.'

'I'm sorry?' Craning myopic gold-hoop ear so little stirrup bones may waggle, the cracked vibration of my voice.

'Me too.' I move her bones and pay my fine for loan of towel and guarantee that it won't be me that breaks the rules of house displayed in foot-high letters red like Lenin on the wall.

And then in bunk bed cell I crouch and too late hear that strangled call: Get Out! Run! Escape! As though with every faltered thump my heart has told me all along: 'Go not into the Millhouse, Fool, for 'tis a miserable purgatory all.'

I Wake Again
In sorry state I wake again,
through midday's faceless clamour crawl,
to shower numb in lukewarm soap
and mark the weakness of it all.
To move but not remove the filth,
for through the bricked-up lint I hear,
the hollow next-door sex slap-slap
and wash myself in dread and fear.
In cleanliness both lean and false
then struggles on this strangled ewe.
To find what safety lies in three
and huddle with the other two
On couches cramped and sunken dust,
the world to slaughter me must strive,
for in among the gap-year chaff
are sitting not my two, but five.
I gasp and baulk, I stifle retch,
and yawning cracks around me grow,
for watching me with naughty eyes
is frizzy-headed Mandy Stowe...

24: Alright?

'Alright?' she says, watching me, waiting for a reaction, waiting for me to tell her how to react. I am emotionless. Or maybe I am so emotional that any single emotion is drowned in a swamp of others.

'Yeah,' I manage, hugging Beth and Amy and finally Mandy. It isn't unpleasant to see her. In the month or so we've been apart, as I've stumbled through Patagonia with Matty and Aaron, most of the bad feelings have been evaporated in the mist of booze, coke and long bus journeys. This unlooked-for meeting is just another straw on today's already staggering haystack hump. I don't need any more surprises.

We sit and chat, but I'm absent. My eyes flicker around restlessly. The room is a hot potato, concentrating on one thing for too long burns.

Around us pink-clean youths in carefully carefree clothing bray loudly in middle-class English, each trying desperately to be overheard by the others, each screaming in body and neatly messed hair 'Notice me! Notice me!'

'When did you get here?' asks Mandy, still watching me, defensiveness swinging slightly towards concern.

'This morning.' I know she already knows, she just doesn't know what else to say. My expression is one long wince, my shoulders hover beside my ears, my back bowed.

The conversation continues, I am part of it but I'm not listening. Somewhere inside me a voice asks: *Are you okay, Wil?* And suddenly I'm concerned for myself, suddenly I feel too close to madness. I thought my mood was a product of last night's bus trip and the rum and the beer and the evil memories which flash up now and then like dead leaves in a stream. Memories of being already spinning-drunk, playing cards in the Puerto Medryn bus terminal in honour of Aaron's birthday. Dim, guilty flashes of outbursts rude and obnoxious towards those Argentinean guys on the bus. The way Matty and Aaron looked at me when I came to, as if my bullish, cocksure self might have stuck around.

I thought that this morning's stagger though the city and the Millhouse's pre-packed, hygienic unfriendliness was to blame for the emptiness I feel now, the sheepishness, but now I'm beginning to worry that this sour detachment might be something else, something deeper, something more permanent; the weeks of excess and self-inflicted brain damage finally catching up with me.

I need to get out. I need air. I need peace. I need safety.

'I'm going to get a hair cut,' I say, too quickly, getting up too fast like a drunk about to puke. The others stop talking and look at me. 'I'm fine,' I say before they can ask, and I lurch away.

As soon as the door closes behind me and I'm back in South America I feel better. I stand in the alley, light a cigarette and pull my hood up against the drizzle. When I finish the first one I light another, standing there in the alley with the cars and umbrellas passing, feeling the rain on my face, staring blankly through namby-pamby backpackers buzzing endlessly in and out of the Millhouse. I finish the second cigarette and start walking. I walk up one block and then the next, cars zipping past me on the filmy street, newspaper stands under dripping trees, ragged kids juggling at the traffic lights. When I get to the end of the next block I just keep walking, briefly noting where I live, barely noticing where I'm going.

After half an hour the numbness in my brain clears enough for my body to feel the cold. A few blocks after that I pass a barbershop and remember why I came out. I turn back and duck inside out of the rain, stomping the drips off my clothes. When I look up I feel as if I've walked fifty years back in time. There is nothing in the room, apart from me, which suggests I'm not in the 1950s. The ceiling is high and nicotine-stained, black-beamed and dusty. A ceiling fan hangs limply still and broken, trailing cobwebs and age. On the white-tiled walls, curling and dog-eared, old black and white posters hang; grimy flat tops and crew cuts, partings and wispy, fading smiles.

Beside threadbare leather-cushioned recliners stand the two barbers, white-coated and watching me with mild amusement as if it is me who looks strange. Both are bald, both are in their sixties and both are as timeless as the room in which they stand.

'*Buenos dias, Señor,*' they say together.

'*Buenos,*' I say. Neither makes a move to offer me a seat, it is my choice.

I take off my hoodie and hang it on the hook by the door, already moving slower, already merging with the antiquity of this little rabbit hole snow dome I've walked into. I sit in the seat nearest to me and watch in the mildewed mirror as my chosen barber smirks at his mate and deftly flicks a white sheet over my head and tucks it under my chin.

'*¿Que quieres, Señor?*' He asks with mock politeness, bowing slightly. His mate smirks.

'*Todo numero dos, por favor,*' I rattle off my pigeon explanation for how I like my head shaved. Both of them roll their eyes at my lack of imagination and begin tapping and pointing at the soggy old posters on the wall. Perhaps I'd like a short back and sides? No, thank you, just a number two please. Perhaps a side-parting with pomade and a flick? Again, thank you but no. Are you sure? Yes, thank you, quite sure. Sulkily they roll their eyes again. I feel almost guilty enough to let them have their way. But not quite.

The three of us are quiet for a while, my chosen barber concentrates on my hair, the other flicks though a brittle-paged magazine he's probably flicked through a thousand times before. I sit happily in my comfy chair, my mind on nothing but the room reflected in the mirror, the tranquillity of it, the fact that I've never been in a place so perfectly ancient and yet still so alive and functional.

'Where are joo from?' asks the one not cutting my hair, laying down the magazine and talking to my reflection.

'*Soy Gales*,' I answer in Spanish. 'I'm Welsh.'

'Ooh!' says my barber, his eyes widening, still taking the piss. '*¿Gales* eh? *¿Te gusto los Ingles*? Do you like the English?'

I laugh and tell him that historically we hate the English more than anyone else does, but personally I quite like a few of them. They look disappointed at my fairness so I tell them that I'd go out of my way to burn down the Houses of Parliament, Tony Blair and all, given half a chance. This they applaud and they grin and for the first time they stop taking the piss out of me for a second.

'What do joo think about Argentina?' my barber asks, fishing for compliments. I tell him I love it. I tell him that it reminds me of home. Though unlike home, I tell him, the women are more beautiful, the wine is superb and the beef is the best in the world.

He finishes up and brushes me down and tells me I'm welcome back any time. I shake them both by the hand and leave a tip on the marble sideboard. Then I pull on my damp hoodie and step back outside, into the rain and the rising gloom and the twenty-first century.

I feel better. At least I don't feel numb any more. The hair caught down the back of my neck is irritating. So is the thought of going back to the Millhouse and Mandy.

Why is she here? What does she want from me? I was a bastard to her and I felt guilty, then I let it all go and I was back on the road to Happy Wil. I know I've been a bit of a bad drunk, but that's understandable. I want an easy life. What possible good could there be in this? In the return of the arsehole? The return of compromise and self-delusion?

I shudder. I need to find another place to live. I need to not do this Mandy thing again. I need to avoid it at all cost because I'm fragile and the consequences could be disastrous.

I'm walking again, smoking, hood up, head down, probably talking to myself too. I need some grounding. I need some advice.

I stop at an internet café and order a coffee and a computer. It's a shiny place made of plastic and fake wood veneer, name tags and bad patterned carpets.

What's happened to the world? I find myself wondering. Then I tell myself to stop being such an old man.

There's an e-mail from mum telling me how the garden looks and who's dead and who's had a baby. There's one from Delores telling me she's back in the States and the man she loves doesn't love her. And there's one from Lucy. She's in Buenos Aires looking for a job as an English teacher. She says she's staying in a hostel called the Orange Tree, but she doesn't say where it is.

I reply to all three e-mails in the same, melodramatic, melancholy tone – insisting at the end of each that I'm okay. That there really isn't any reason to worry about me – a cry for help if ever I made one. I consider calling home, but it would be early morning on a Tuesday and I don't fancy the distracted gaiety of my morning mum's conversation. There's nothing for it but to finish my coffee, smile gratitude at the name-tagged polo shirt at the front desk and keep walking.

I steer clear of modernity and head down back streets, through crumbling cobbled plazas and one-block parks of gnarled trees and bum-sprawled benches. There's something Parisian about the streets and houses here, a crookedness, a lusty, brooding decrepitude. It makes me feel brave and almost invisible, romantic in a dreary, down-and-out way. My trainers squeak in time with my steps, the puddles splash in rhythm.

Night is falling by the time I feel ready to face it all again so I turn right and head for the rumble of the massive, eighteen lane highway which bisects the centre of the city. Finding it, I turn right again and head back towards the Millhouse. I have a plan now, a plan and a feeling that, though the winds of life may blow me where they will, I can always just pull up my hood and walk until I find the ground beneath my feet and a bit of reality on which to anchor my soul.

My plan is simple: I'll stay another night in cellblock M. I'll be polite and pleasant to Mandy, but keep her at arm's length and then I'll escape tomorrow morning, to find Lucy and the Orange Tree, or someplace else to stay. Perhaps it's time to spend some time alone again. Perhaps I can play at being normal for a while and see if I can't make a habit of it.

If I throw enough shit around some of it is bound to stick, somewhere, sometime.

25: 'And behind you, I have warned you, there are awful things.' Will Oldham

I sleep the night in fitful dreams, the air clogged with the boozy farts of my neighbours, their feet three feet from my head, the sounds of innocent debauchery echoing up the stairwells. I wake still full of my plan. Escape. Run. Get out.

I shower and brush teeth in bemused wonder at the sounds of violent sex still seeping through the sweaty bathroom walls.

Are they just prolific fuckers, or are there lots of them doing shift work?

My reflection doesn't know. He blinks back at me purple-eyed, toothpaste around his mouth.

Are they still going since yesterday morning or is it just coincidence that they fuck loudly every time I go to the bathroom?

My reflection doesn't care. The disgust I feel for them is just another reason to escape, a dirty catalyst fuelling my plan. Get out. Run.

Matty and Aaron are snoring still, surrounded by the five other occupants of our boys-only dorm, like pirates in haggis-sagging hammocks, stinking and muttering. I dress and plod downstairs into the windowless bowels of the hostel, my mind twitching and convulsing with the energy of the place, the cavernous production line design, the feeling that we're all just lambs bound for the block, or the bolt gun, or whatever vile means they'll employ to do us in once they've fleeced us all.

I find an empty table in the prison-like mess hall and eat my bread, cheese and sausage, my arms instinctively circling my tray, my head bent, eyes watchful. I must look like a psycho. I certainly feel like a psycho.

'D'you mind if we sit here?' Two of them, Northern accents, early twenties, acne, polyester.

'Go ahead' sounds like 'go away'. I find myself disappointed that they don't think I'm a psycho. That makes me feel even more like a psycho.

'Where you from?' asks one. I'm tempted to lie. Palestine. Uzbekistan.

'North Wales.' Better try and be friendly. Don't want to be a psycho. Remember the plan. Normal, normal, normal.

'What footie team d'you support?' asks the other one.

'Liverpool,' I answer, as I always have. Ian Rush. John Barnes. Ronnie Whelan. *Why the fuck is he asking me that?*

'Where are you watching the match?' asks the first. White bread sandwich, cheese and onion crisps.

'What match?' I ask. They exchange a look. That same 'fucking hippy' look I used to get when the kids at school would ask me if I'd seen Inspector Gadget, or The A Team.

No TV. Home-knit jumpers. Home-made bread. No hire purchase. No lace curtains.

'The Champions League final,' says the second, indulging me, pitying me, 'Liverpool/AC Milan.'

'Oh shit,' says me, mouth full of bread and cheese. 'I've been a bit out of touch. What time's kick off?'

Kick off is at three thirty. Six hours away. I could move house and settle in and still have time to find a bar and watch the game. But Matty and Aaron and the rest of them are asleep so I can't pack yet. Better just hang out and wait for them.

I hang out and wait, trying to read, but it's not Matty and Aaron who arrive bleary eyed. It's Mandy Stowe.

'Alright?' she asks, rubbing the bleary from her eyes and yawning. 'Where did you get to yesterday?'

'Just around,' I say, dog-earing the same page I've been trying to read for half an hour, laying the book on my knee. 'Sleep well?'

'Yeah,' she says, flopping down next to me on the couch, 'got drunk with Matty and Aaron and the girls. You okay?'

'I guess so,' says me, calm all of a sudden, relaxed with her for the first time in a long time. Good to have someone to talk to. 'I'm just a bit lost in my head. Too much booze and drugs and travelling. It gets a bit much, moving all the time.'

'Tell me about it,' she says and stretches her arms over her head and as she stretches I notice her tits.

S'bin a while.

'Me and Amy have been having a mental time. Just partying constantly.'

'You seen Lucy?' I ask, looking her in the eye, feeling horny and screaming at myself at the same time to keep her at arm's length, to remember the plan, *remember the plan!*

'Nah,' she says, matching my look and holding it. We sit

like that for a moment, just staring at each other, saying nothing, my insides tingling, balls tightening.

'Right,' I say, sitting up quickly, tearing myself away from the ball of static building up between us, swallowing the well of saliva in my mouth.

'What you up to?' she asks and I can hear a little mockery in her voice, a little I-know-you-still-want-me.

'I'm gonna get out of this shite hole,' I say, waving my finger at the Slaughterhouse, saying it like she's included in it. Then a little softer, because she doesn't warrant such condemnation: 'I'm going to find a bar, watch Liverpool win the Champions League and get drunk.'

'Oh shit, that's today isn't it?' she says, the mockery gone, retreating a step, back to pleasant and relaxed. 'Want some company?'

And we look into each other's eyes again and I know it's not in the rules to say no, even though everything sensible in me is telling me to do so.

'Yeah,' I say distractedly and then, to make it sound a bit more sincere, I say 'yeah, that'd be nice. It's been a while.'

It's a dull, grey day again outside. The traffic roars and we rush though it, our little taxi a mere drip in the foaming river of cars, trucks and motorbikes. Matty's with us, sitting up front, asking the driver about the picture of a little girl and a woman smiling on the dashboard.

Mandy and I sit in the back seat. The pair of us wanting to touch but not touching. Knowing from habit what the other feels like and smells like and wanting it but knowing also how bad it was when it turned sour. How it's better to forgo the touching and keep a clear head and an anxiety-free heart.

'*Aqui es bien, gracias,*' I tell the driver. He pulls up outside the walled graveyard in Recoleta, the same graveyard in which

Eva Peron's body lies. Madonna, rotting in a mildewed ball gown, weeds in her gappy teeth. Plaster angels gathering moss, praying with blind, sandy eyes. Cracked marble and mouldy carnations.

The sports bar across the cobbled street is an insult to it all. As tacky and as misguided as Madonna cast as Evita, as wantonly vile as McDonald's furniture or Planet Hollywood; a temple to television and polished aluminium, but on a hundred screens the game has already kicked off and we have no choice but to enter.

We sit at the bar on high stools and watch the game on a screen above the bar staff's heads, drinking beers at first in excitement and then in dread, then in desperation, yelling obscenities at Milan, at Liverpool and at any barman unlucky enough to get in the way.

By half-time and three-nil I'm drunk again and muttering, along with everyone else: *it's just a game, it's not important, it's just a game.*

Sitting next to us is a broad, sandy-haired man in a suit with whom, throughout the first half, I'd shared looks of exasperation and disgust. When I come back from the toilet, the half-time commentary blaring from the sound system, he's chatting to Mandy and sharing his squid rings with Matty.

His name is Scott, this sandy-haired suit, an investment executive or something; a rich Yorkshireman and, though he seemed a bit suspect at first, a good man too.

'What're you drinking Scott?' I ask, camaraderie strengthened in loss, in common distaste at Liverpool's sorry performance.

'Beer,' is the answer, beer is what I buy, four of them, each at the price of a six pack in the supermarket, my credit card and Liverpool so far in the red it no longer seems to matter.

The second half kicks off. At three-one hope starts growing

like seedlings in Evita's skull. At three-two I fall off my stool and gash my shin. At three-three the four of us are hugging like beer-soaked family and crying like drunken babies.

And when our Steve lifts the cup, half an hour later and half a world away, it is us who are the victors. It is us who won it for them, we are the champions, us. By the time we make it back to the Millhouse we have a bottle of champagne each, a cigar and a love for each other that is undying and all-encompassing.

They're not even nearly ready for us, we glorious four. Pain and the plan lie where I threw them, paranoia and wretchedness too. What remains is a glorious, bullish blur, the like of which has never been seen before or since. The Millhouse is holding a salsa class.

The globe spins regardless and for an hour or two we spin with it, Scott in his suit and us in our glorious rags, cigars in our mouths, champers in our fists and a contempt for all in our path. A contempt for the prim properness of the lousy, scared backpackers. 'Get out, you fuckers!' I want to scream. 'Get out of your bubbles, get out of your minds, forget this nonsense, this "safety" this "security". Get out and live, grab the bull by the horns and fuck his snotty nostrils. Bleed and draw blood! Fuck and get fucked! Fuck life! Fuck death! Throw yourselves away and LET FUCKING GO!'

It's not a pretty speech, but somehow it shines with pure justification. It is bright-eyed disregard for sanity and the enforced sanitary order of the hostel. It's a big 'Fuck You!' to all that's neat and pretty in the world and most of all it's a big 'Fuck You!' to my plan. What the fuck do I care for normality when I can shine as bright as any anglerfish's eye and tell this murky world to go fuck itself?

Then a new plan occurs to me: I must consummate my reversal in philosophy. I must live by my word. I must fuck life.

In the stairwell I grab Mandy by the hand and ram my tongue down her throat. Then I drag her to the bathroom and in among the Toilet Duck and Mister Músculo we reunite. For an hour the thumping sex sounds are our sounds. Ours is the loveless fight-fucking, the sport-sex frustration burn panting spreadeagled friction. Ours, all of it is ours...

And then it is gone. In an echoing instant all that is left of my triumphant war against the world is sour sweat and scraped knees. All I have left is me. White of arse and shrunken bruised of cock. Guilty and sorry. Full from arse to elbow with regret and shame.

26: The Orange Tree

The next morning is one of the worst. It is pitiless, I am pitiful, and the world and Buenos Aires feels like it might never be right again. Everything hurts and everything is black. Not black in a nice sense either. It is black like dread, black like the fear dogs can sense, or rapists in the park. Black like drowning in a pool of centipedes.

There are cracks in the blackness though, There are handholds and footholds in the slippery abyss. But they are few... precious few.

First there is darkness and in the darkness lurks everything dark, me, and even darker things besides. Some of them are memories, some of them are shame and others are homesickness and desolation. Then there is bad coffee and the never-ending grunts and moans of the bathroom nymphomaniacs...

Then there is the outside world for a minute and that stinks too. There is the block-long howling-road stumble to the shop and the awkward eye-avoiding mumble for Rizla and chocolate milk. Then the first faint glow of light appears; like a firefly in a whale's black gut. The shopkeeper asks me if I'm okay. I tell him I am not and the only other customer apart from myself laughs at me. That isn't the glow. The glow comes when the shopkeeper asks me where I'm from and I tell him I'm Welsh. He nearly leaps over the counter to hug me.

'I love the Welsh!' He roars at me in Spanish.

'My life hurts,' I reply.

'You are my family,' he roars at me.

'I'm going now,' I reply.

'Come back soon, my brother,' he roars at me.

'Okay,' I reply and I leave. All the way down the block I can hear him roaring after me: '*Viva Gales! Viva Gales! Viva Argentina!*'

Despite myself I have to smile. That is the first crack of light in the darkness. The next crack of light comes about an hour later. I find a map that tells me where the Orange Tree is. It is just across the highway from the Millhouse. Five minutes away, across eighteen lanes of traffic and six sets of traffic lights. It has been there all along.

I suppose leaving the Slaughterhouse is good, though it doesn't feel that way. I don't like the bill they make me pay, the bill for all that booze I don't remember drinking, the bill for borrowing a towel. What kind of hostel charges you for borrowing a towel? What kind of hostel doesn't let you have girls in your bed? What kind of hostel has more rules than Soviet Russia? The Slaughterhouse.

The next shaft of light comes a few seconds after my release. A flash of realisation, a flash of clarity: Next door to the Millhouse is a porno cinema. I hadn't really noticed it before, but now it all makes sense – the phantom bathroom fuckers weren't actually fuckers at all. They were just the recorded sounds of fuckers past, leeching through the seedy walls, the by-products of dirty old men invading my world and not some unnaturally, wickedly prolific fuckers. This realisation fills me with a palpable sense of relief because, in a sane world, it would have been impossible for anyone to have such violent, loud sex for so long. Perhaps there is a little sanity left in the world after all.

Then there is Matty. Matty, my slippery foothold brethren, who helps me lug my gear to the Orange Tree, who helps me cross the miles and miles of traffic lights and zebra crossings, who helps me press the doorbell and helps me up the stairs.

And as soon as I pass the threshold I know I've climbed out of the blackness. As soon as I see the open fire, the tattered couches and the lime-green walls, I know I have evolved. As soon as I see Lucy sitting with her crew by the fire with a newspaper and a glass of red wine I know that this tadpole has grown legs and become a frog. I know too that a frog is just one step away from being a prince, if he can just get the right girl to pucker up.

'Willy!' that bonnie wee Scots lass cries, and, though I know she isn't the one to make me royalty, this frog hops up and flops down next to her and nearly croaks his final croak.

'Where have you been?' she asks after a long and well-needed hug. 'When did you get here? What happened?'

'S'bin horrible,' I groan, though I smile as well.

'What has?'

'The Millhouse,' I whimper. Lucy and her friends exchange knowing looks and no more is said until I have my pack on a bunk, my name in the book, a glass of wine in one hand and a spliff in the other.

So here I am, back in the land of the living, tarred and scarred but on the way up, reunited with an old buddy and being introduced to new ones. They've heard about me, apparently.

'This is Willy,' says Lucy with pride and a pat on the knee.

'Hey guys.'

'This is lovely Tim,' she continues, nodding towards a short, dark-haired man with a big smile. 'He's Canadian. We love him.'

'Hello lovely Tim,' I shake his little hand.

'This is lovely Mylo. He and Tim are best mates. He's from Canada as well.'

'Hello lovely Mylo,' I shake his big, red hand. He also has a big red face, a big friendly grin, big clumpy walking boots and a little brown goatee. He looks like a big, stoned, inflatable Scooby.

'This is lovely Pete,' says Lucy, putting her hand on my shoulder and pointing me at a medium sized guy with blond hair and a baseball cap. We shake hands. 'He's from South Africa, Tim and Mylo picked him up somewhere in Brazil.'

'Like herpes,' says Tim.

'Uh-huh-huh-huh,' chuckles Mylo.

'Is everyone lovely?' I ask.

'Yes,' says Lucy.

'Good,' says me.

And then that first crackle of energy seems to die and we all just stare into the fire for a while.

'We've all been up for three days,' says Lucy after a while.

'I got some sleep yesterday,' says Mylo proudly.

'Lightweight,' says Tim.

'Oh shit,' I groan, realising that this frog has just hopped out of the frying pan and right into the fire. 'Can anyone sell me some weed?'

Even in a sizzling skillet a man can sleep – if he has a mind to, if he's tired and stoned enough. Sleep with the roar and boom of the highway outside bouncing through the room, sleep in the sweat of old booze and adrenaline, sleep in half dreams and blur, sleep until midday light and loud and then awake. Awake and clear and coffee and shower. Awake and breakfast and start the day on a good foot, a clean slate. And then to build upon it.

Then there is the darkened TV room, just to see who's doing what, just to see what's happening today. Two men looking like they haven't slept in days is what's happening today. Two men dishevelled and wild eyed. Two men watching American sitcoms, not laughing.

'Morning!' I say happily, and stand beside the crusty couch and watch a second of awkward domesticity. It's not funny. The two men turn and look at me and blink with cracked, red eyes.

'Good morning,' says one in thick Slavic accent.

'Good morning,' says the other in soft Aussie.

'You guys are looking a bit rough,' says me, enjoying the fact that I'm not.

'Do you want line?' asks the Slav, enjoying the fact that I'll say no.

Why not? I think.

'Why not,' I say.

They look at each other and then they look at me.

'Good man,' says the Aussie.

'Good man, yes,' says the Slav, and he reaches into his pocket and brings out an envelope sized wrap and chops up three heaps on the stained coffee table. He rolls a note, bangs one line into his head in one vicious snort and grins at me. Then he passes the note to the Aussie who tests both nostrils to find the least blocked and winces as he does. The Aussie's line disappears into his head and he rubs his face and groans. I take the note from him and test my own nostrils. I decide on the left one and roll the note a little tighter. Then I bend over the table and push it into my nostril, letting it unroll slightly to fill the hole. Then, as much like the Slav as I can,

I inhale quickly, holding my other nostril shut. I manage half the line before I have to stop. I grin and switch nostrils and finish the rest, licking my finger, wiping the residue off the table and rubbing it on my gums.

Instantly my nasal passages are numb, quickly the rest of my face starts to tingle, my heart speeds up, my breathing sweetens and a well of excitement fills my guts.

'Thanks lads,' The world is already different enough to make my voice sound odd. 'That's some *strong* shit!'

'You are welcome,' says the Slav. 'It is the fucking shit.'

He sounds funny, swearing in his almost-Russian accent. I grin.

'I'm Wil,' I hold out my hand.

'Marko.' The Slav takes my hand and shakes it gravely.

'Paul.' The Aussie shakes my hand too. Both of their hands are cold and clammy, like cellars on a hot day. They turn back to the sitcom. A fat American kid is fighting hilariously with his sister. The audience is in stitches. It's still not even remotely funny. I have to get out.

'I have to get out,' I say to them and they look at me like I've got it all wrong. 'I got some sleep last night,' I explain as I leave the room.

Lucy isn't up yet. Mylo the Canadian and Pete the South African are; their faces are puffy and red.

'Get any sleep?' I ask then cheerily.

'Yeah!' says Mylo happily. 'I guess we all just crashed out.'

'Yah,' Pete says in his mellow, clipped accent, 'I suppose it just caught up with us.'

'What're you all up to today?' I ask, feeling giddier and giddier by the minute, my enthusiasm for life just bursting out of me.

'Might smoke a joint,' says Mylo.

'Yah,' says Pete, 'that would be cool.'

Up on the roof the sun is bright and warm. I lean against the low parapet wall and watch the road below. It is huge, huge and roaring. I watch the jugglers at the traffic lights and the policemen on the corner. I look down the cleavage of a woman on the pavement below.

'I can see your tits,' I say to her. She can't hear me. Mylo and Pete lean next to me.

'Where?' asks Mylo. I point. He chuckles.

'We can see your tits,' says Pete.

Mylo passes me the joint. It's short and fat with no roach – North American style, pure and tickly. We sit quietly on the warm roof tar and smile at the sun.

'Some crazy Slavic guy gave me a line for breakfast,' I say absently, enjoying the excitement in my diaphragm.

'Marko?' asks Mylo.

'Mmmm.' I nod slowly.

'Good shit,' says Pete.

'Mmmm.'

We finish the joint and chat about where we've been and where we're going. I'm stoned now so the coke is mellowed. Mellowed but still racing like wasps through my veins.

'Shall we drink a beer?' asks Mylo after a while.

'Yah,' says Pete, 'we better had.'

I smile and agree too. Somehow this fire I've leapt into doesn't seem half as bad as the frying pan I leapt out of. Happy little frog…

There's a pool table in one of the hostel's many rooms and a fridge full of cold beers. There's a little book to keep tabs and a hotdog take-away downstairs. There are about twenty of us staying here and nearly all of us know each other. There's a feeling of camaraderie, a collective love of debauchery, a trust and a common, unconditional forgiveness for all fuck ups and freak outs. This is the kind of place you could get lost in, the kind of place to lose it and find it again and maybe even realise that 'it' never existed at all.

The Orange Tree is the Millhouse's antithesis – a free place, a loving place and, best of all, a place almost devoid of rules. There is a blackboard in the main reception area on which someone has scrawled a list of dos and don'ts in a dusty, primary school hand. Tim says that they are there to be broken and should never, under any circumstances, be adhered to. The receptionist looks up from her magazine and smiles agreement.

'Just don't fuck with me,' she says.

In the pool room we roll joints, drink cold beers and eat hot dogs. At some point someone suggests we should leave the hostel. The suggestion is ignored.

Occasionally I wonder where Matty and Aaron and the others are and I feel a little guilty for not introducing them to the scene. Occasionally I wonder where Mandy is and I shudder at the mental image of the bathroom and our violent fucking.

It's safe here. I'm safe here. I'll go and find them tomorrow. I'm too fucked up to go anywhere now. The world just wouldn't understand me...

The next day I wake up at noon feeling fuzzy and rattled by the booze, the coke and the bass throb of traffic from outside. I also feel guilty. I feel guilty for abandoning the others in the Slaughterhouse. I feel guilty for having had such a good time without them. We were a good team, Matty, Aaron and me. I owe them a lifeline. Perhaps I owe them more than that, but an introduction to the Orange Tree will do.

I shower in cold water, gasping and goose-pimpling and shivering awake. Then I dress and cross the road to the

Millhouse. None of them are up yet so I sit and drink chocolate milk and smoke cigarettes.

It's only been a couple of days since I was here, but already the place is full of new backpackers I don't recognise. I wonder how they all remain so innocent looking and clean. They seem to drink as much as the rest of us. Coke is so common back home that they must do plenty of it. They seem to have travelled. They must have had some rough times like the rest of us. So why is there so much innocence in their eyes? Why are they so soft looking? Why do I feel so tired and jaded in comparison? What makes me feel so different?

'What's on your mind Wil?' Matty must have sneaked up on me; he's standing beside me, hair still wet from the shower. I'm staring at a group of backpackers laughing at a table, my jaw slack, my cigarette needs ashing and the carton of chocolate milk in my hand is in danger of spilling.

'Oh! Alright Matty?' I snap out of it, ash on the floor and rub it into the tiles with my toe. 'I was just pondering the nature of innocence. What you up to?'

'I've just got up, mate,' he sits down next to me, locking his hands behind his head. 'What you up to?'

'I came to rescue you guys from this nest of candyfloss snakes,' I point at the room with my chocolate milk.

'Why thank you kind sir,' Matty laughs and then rubs his eyes with the balls of his hands and says in a serious voice. 'If we come I guess the girls will come too and you know what that means, don't you?'

'Mandy,' says me. 'I knows it.'

'You sure you want to do that to yourself?'

'No.'

'We've got to get out of here though,' he says, looking about. 'Do you know how much they charge for a beer?'

'Don't want to. I came to see if you wanted to come over

to the promised land, not to discuss local economics.'

'Whatever. I'll go and wake Aaron up and see what he wants to do.'

'I'll make my way back over there,' I throw my empty carton at a bin and miss by a mile. 'You know where it is, don't you?'

'Sure, I'll see you in a bit.'

'Peace,' I call over my shoulder and give the CCTV camera the finger as I leave.

Hours later. I'm stoned again. Drunk and stoned and playing pool. Lucy is out looking for a job. Mylo and Tim are eating hot dogs. Various other people are drinking, or smoking or snorting coke. The hostel feels like an old opium den or a halfway crack-house: friendly but slightly deranged. Normality belongs to none of us, so normality is no longer the norm. It's an odd feeling, a feeling made more odd by the buzz of the door bell and the entrance of Matty, Aaron, Beth, Amy and Mandy, packs and all, straight and almost healthy compared to the rest of us. In they bounce. Hellos they chorus and I swim through it all, introducing them to members of the Crackhouse, catching Beth and Amy's looks of distaste at the amount of drugs and booze floating about, Matty and Aaron's too.

It's odd – suddenly I'm the connection between these two worlds. When I invited my old crew over I hadn't imagined there'd be much difference between them and the new crew. Seeing them merge makes me realise how stark the comparison actually is.

Maybe that's why I don't feel innocent; I've broken down my capacity to be shocked or disgusted, made callous my ability to differentiate between that which is pure and that which is morally corrupt.

'What's the matter, Wil?' It's Mandy. I must have zoned out again, vacantly staring at the spliff in my hand.

'Oh hey Mandy,' I say, a little too warmly, 'nothing's the

matter. I was just thinking about stuff.'

'I've been doing lots of thinking too,' she cocks her head to one side, watching me.

'Oh yeah?' the warmth is almost gone. 'What you been thinking about?'

She hears the edge in my voice, that little change of tone warning her to stay back. I didn't even mean to be nasty, it just slipped out that way.

'Nothing,' she clams up, straightens her head and clenches her jaw. We sit in silence. I really hate being like this. It's so petty and yet it feels so immovable and ever present.

'Sorry M,' I say, trying to shift the unshiftable tension between us, 'I didn't get much sleep last night. I'm just grumpy.'

If I could just be honest and tell her how I really feel we could probably get over this nonsense. But I'm not really sure how I feel and I'm too stoned and too far down the road of bullshit to make any difference now. Might as well just pretend to be friendly and ball up the guilt and anger in my guts until it explodes at some point. I laugh out loud at myself for thinking that, staring into the distance and chuckling.

'What?' asks Mandy.

'Nothing,' I say, and that makes it ten times worse. Now, instead of just being dishonest I'm being secretive as well.

What the fuck is she doing here? I ask myself, not for the first time.

She likes you, comes the answer.

But why? Surely I've been so horrible to her she's got the message by now. God I'm such a cunt – why can't I just be honest and tell her to go away?

Because you're scared. Because you're weak. Because you're losing it.

'You alright?' she asks. My inner dialogue must have been showing in my expressions.

'Yeah,' I lie, 'just a bit stoned.'

'You got any weed?' she asks.

'Yeah.'

'Wanna go smoke a joint?'

'Yeah. Okay.'

I am a sucker for punishment. A sucker indeed. And the worst thing about it is I don't do this innocently. I lead myself, with eyes open, into trap after trap and complain every time I get stuck.

Forgive me father, for I know exactly what I do.

27: 'We've come a long way from migrating crustaceans.' Mike Ladd

Time passes quickly. We pick the bones of nights out well into vulturous mornings. Snarling, blood-caked muzzles and clenched jaws lick cracked lips with hyperactive tongues, leaving behind nothing but dry bones and crackling skin.

We hibernate our days away. The few who keep normal hours are growled at and despised for the painful shadows of comparison they cast upon us. We rise to squint warily at an hour or two of murky daylight. Breakfast is dinner is time to wind up this carousel again and continue the vicious cycle of pleasure snatched from the jaws of pain, of suffering masked thinly by endorphins wrung out of tired souls.

Muffled sniffs and snuffles emanate from every bathroom, the groans and coughs not long ceased, the dry retching forgotten but not gone. This feeding frenzy the only way to be free of racking pain and yawning guilt pulled down upon us solely by our rotten selves.

We are stranded here, marooned by our inability to ever come down. Too fucked to get off the ride. Too fucked up to ride at any other speed than a shuffling limp. Too numb to care. Or too scared.

These are dark days my children, dark days indeed.

But soon our pennies will run out; soon the ride must end. We will find ourselves blinking at the morning sun like newborn hyenas, unsure who we are or how we got here. The twitches and convulsions will gradually cease and the cheap fairground that is life will once again open its gaudy gates and usher us in.

We will slowly pan out from this microcosm in which we exist and the full, comforting, familiar horror of the world will again press us into conformity, stretch us too thin to care and fill in the pits of self-disgust with mundane normality and mild self-hatred.

But for now, my infant nightlings, let the organ grinder dust off his cracked organ and gently fuck us into yet another night of sour adrenaline and dripping, caustic oblivion. Let the dust settle once again in our raw sinuses. Let the veins in our temples begin their merry, throbbing dance. Let our jaws begin their trembling race.

Come, my little ones, for the ride is winding up, come clamp your crooked claws once more into its crusted mane.

For darker things await the ones we leave behind.

And darker things than this could break us all.

28: 'Have you thought that you might waste away?
   You don't care much for yourself.
   There are circles deep beneath your eyes.
   Why must you do this to yourself?'

Bonnie 'Prince' Billy

The memories are dim, they swim up almost to the surface and then they disappear again, lost in ripples and warps of dreams and confusion. I remember lots of screaming and a frenzied, hustling activity but it's blurred, just shapes and colours. Then there is Matty and Lucy screaming at me to go to bed. Forcing me into the dorm. Why are they so hysterical?

There is a pain in my left shoulder and my right hand is stuck to the sheets. From the ache in my knuckles I assume it is blood sticking me to the bed. I won't move yet. I don't think I'm still bleeding...

I lie there with my left arm over my eyes, groaning. Bass waves from trucks and buses outside bounce about the room, vibrating my eardrums and rattling my eyelids. I feel like I'm in an oil tanker. Seasick and scurvied. *What the fuck happened last night?*

According to my memory: Nothing much.

According to my knuckles and shoulder: Something.

I check my face with my left hand. If I was fighting I must have done pretty well. There isn't a scratch on my face.

Was I fighting?

I feel like death, but I have to find out. Shower first. Then coffee. Then I'll find out.

Before all that I have to unstick my stuck knuckles from the sheet. I should soak it. Nothing to soak it with. I'll just have to peel it away.

I hold the sheet with my left hand and pull my right towards me. It stings but it comes away clean. The sound of it almost makes me retch.

Last night we were drinking. Then we took some coke. None of that is unusual. I was pissed off. Pissed off at myself. Pissed off because of Mandy. She was sitting alone. Drinking red wine in the corner. Talking to herself. Her eyes were red and puffy, focused on nothing.

Talking to herself.

I'm responsible.

She's going crazy and I'm responsible.

I bring my right hand out from under the covers. The two

largest knuckles are a wreck of twisted skin and dried blood. My whole hand is swollen. I move my fingers one by one, wincing and biting my lip. Nothing broken. Just bruises.

What did I do?

I stand by the side of my bunk, steadying myself with my left hand, looking down at my right, rocking slightly, moaning at the thumping agony of my brain.

I could just leave right now. I could just pack up and get on the next bus out of town. *What have I done?*

I can't leave. Not until I've had a shower. Not until I find out what happened. Maybe then I'll have to leave.

Stop thinking now. Shower.

I don't know what time it is. Morning. Maybe afternoon. The door creaks as I open it. Maria the receptionist looks up. She sees it's me. Her face turns hard, her eyes sad. She shakes her head dolefully and returns to her magazine. 'I'm not angry, I'm just disappointed,' as my mum used to say.

Oh Mum. Oh shit Mum. What have I done?

I resist the temptation to ask Maria what's going on. Shower first. Don't think.

I run the water cold and strip out of my pants. They fall into a puddle on the floor. I watch them soak it up. I do nothing.

I check my left shoulder in the mirror but there isn't a mark on it. Maybe a light bruise but I can't tell. My eyes hurt. My teeth ache. My nostrils are full of dry and crumbling mucus. My reflection hurts. I want to cry.

You did this to yourself.

I suck the self-pity into my guts and climb into the shower. I almost enjoy the punishing cold water on my back and neck. Almost enjoy the gasping urge to get away from it. Almost enjoy forcing myself to stay there and breathe normally. Almost enjoy punishing that weakness in me.

I did this to myself.

My head clears a little but none of the memories I need come back. Only that one hectic image of Matty and Lucy fighting me into the room. But I remember being more confused than angry.

I remember that feeling from years ago. I remember being punched and kicked in the head by two guys. I wasn't scared then either, nor was I angry, just confused.

My knuckles are bleeding red strings onto cracked white tiles, swirling into the plug hole. I want to cry.

But I suck it up instead.

I step out of the shower and stand looking at myself in the mirror. How long have I been here? How many days have I woken up not remembering the night before? All that my memory has is hangovers. Hangovers and the first few beers and lines. And then I wake up.

I look like shit. Purple bags under my eyes. Ribs showing. Dick shrunk from cold water and coke. Hair frizzy and dry. Hand cracked and bloody.

I have to find out what I did. I can't hide.

I dry myself and wrap the towel around my waist. I wring my sopping pants out in the sink and blow the dry snot out of one nostril and then the other.

Then I force a smile at myself. I am on my side. I am with me. Otherwise I'm fucked.

The floor tiles outside the bathroom are cool against the soles of my feet. Dusty. I concentrate on nothing else. I wander into reception and quietly pull a stool up to the desk. I don't say anything. Maria watches me, watches me like she's watching something distasteful crawl out of a hole.

'*Buenos*,' I say, groaning the word.

'Oh Wil,' she says, shaking her head, 'you are fucking crazy, man.'

She says it slowly, emphasising every word evenly. I wince.

'What…' I stumble, look down at my belly button, lick my lips. They taste of toothpaste and stomach acid. 'What… happened?'

'You mean you don't remember?' She raises her thin eyebrows in doubt and then sighs and shakes her head. 'I didn't see much. I just heard about it. You really don't remember?'

'Not much,' I croak, rubbing my temples. 'I remember Lucy and Matty pushing me into the room and telling me to go to bed. *Nada mas.*'

'Who's Matty?' she asks.

'My Australian friend. The one with the hair,' I say impatiently. 'Are you going to tell me what happened?'

'Lucy saved your ass. That's what happened,' she says and looks back down at her magazine. Conversation over. I shrug and sigh. It can't be that bad. Can it? She hasn't chucked me out. *What did I do?*

I dress slowly. Matty is snoring in the bunk below mine. Above him my sheets are crumpled and hanging half off the bed; there's dark blood dried and crusty on them. I'm tempted to wake him up, but I resist the temptation. Better to find out from someone else than suffer his disappointment too.

When I bend down to pull up my trousers a splitting pain punches my head and I nearly retch again. I steady myself, one hand on my bunk and breathe through it. When the nausea subsides I shuffle downstairs and out into the street. It howls with a torrent of horns and engines, and gashes my soul.

I limp to the coffee shop, order a strong black one and limp back upstairs to sit by the cold fireplace and stare at the ceiling.

What happened?

I'm tired of asking myself the same question. I look over at Maria, but she's ignoring me, reading her magazine with her back to me. I have to find out.

I wander over to Lucy's room and knock softly on the door. Nobody answers. I turn the handle, open the door a little and squeeze through. The room is dark and musty. It smells of socks and alcohol leached through sleeping pores. In the dim light I can make out Lucy's sleeping form on the bed. On the bunks surrounding hers I can make out other still shapes: Tom, Fliss and some others, casualties of last night's debauchery. I sit down on Lucy's bed and put my hand on her arm. It's warm and sticky, but not unpleasant. I'm tempted to lie down and go to sleep next to her. To forget about it all. Maybe it'll go away.

Instead I shake her arm a little and call her name. She doesn't even flinch. I shake her a little harder and call louder. She comes swimming to the surface, muttering incoherently. Her first real words are:

'What? Who? What time is it?'

I tell her it's me and I tell her I don't know what time it is. Maybe afternoon. I tell her I don't even know what day it is.

Suddenly she remembers who I am. She stiffens and props herself up quickly on her elbow. When she speaks her voice is clear and awake:

'Jesus Wil,' I can feel her looking at me in the dark. 'What the fuck *happened* to you last night?'

Her tone is odd. She's almost shying away from me. Almost scared.

'I have no idea,' I say humbly, looking down at the silhouettes of my hands. 'I don't really remember anything.'

'You were scary,' she says and there's a hint of worried sympathy in her voice. Just a hint. 'Let me get dressed. I'll be out in a minute.'

I pause. I want more. I want to be told I'm alright. I want to be told I'm loved.

You did this to yourself, says the voice inside me and I grunt myself up off the bed and stand above her for a second until the thumping pain clears from behind my eyes.

'I'll see you in a minute,' I say and wander back to reception. Maria looks up when I pass.

'What did she say?' she asks.

'Nothing yet, she's getting up now.'

Maria sighs and shakes her head again. I can feel anger welling up in me. I want this to stop now. I didn't mean to do what I did. I'm a nice guy. I don't want to hurt anyone.

I push the anger back down and flop onto the couch. My coffee has cooled enough to drink and I light a cigarette after the first sip. The cigarette tastes of chemicals and rotten wood and nausea fills my mouth with saliva. I wash it down with coffee and the next drag isn't so bad. I fight self-pity back down as well and clear my throat to clear my brain. I'm tempted to leave again, just to run and forget it. But I stay where I am and wait for Lucy.

A memory slides into my head. Sometimes memories have colour. This one is yellow. I was coming down the stairs from the roof. Narrow, steep, stone stairs. I was angry then. I fell down the last few steps. I could hardly walk. The world swam and I was angry. The memory slides away again.

Maybe that's when I hurt my shoulder. Why was I so angry? Was it Mandy? She's my only problem here.

Other than myself.

I don't think it was Mandy. I don't think I'd bust myself up about her. It hurts and it's probably the root of this thing, but I doubt if it's the cause.

'Shall we go and get some breakfast?' Lucy is standing beside me. She looks sullen. She's really not happy with me.

'Sure.' I look over at Maria. She's watching us. I drain the last of my coffee and flick my cigarette butt into the fireplace. Then, with my head hung lower than it should hang, I follow

Lucy out of the Orange Tree and into the street

In the café we sit at plastic covered tables and order eggs from the over-friendly waiter. I find myself wanting to punch him in the face. The thought makes me shrink and wail inside. What the fuck is happening to me?

'So what happened?' I ask after a while, biting back the frustrated fear in my voice.

She sighs, tucks her napkin onto her lap and says:

'I don't know how it started. You just came into the room from upstairs and sat down in front of me and Miguel. You didn't say anything, you just sat there looking at him with this crazy look in your eyes.'

Miguel is living in one of the Orange Tree's rooms, working for the owner as a carpenter. He's a tall Argentinean with big hands and a meaty scar on his sallow face. He's the man to go to when you need some green or some white. He's Lucy's new playmate. Apart from the odd business transaction I haven't had much to do with him. He's dangerous but he's a nice enough guy.

'What crazy look? Why?' I ask, cringing with every cell in my body.

'I don't know why. You just sat down and started staring him out. You looked pretty psycho. I asked you if you were okay and you said you were fine. Then you just went on staring at him. I could tell you were wasted from the way you spoke.'

'We were all wasted,'

'Yeah but you were *really* wasted.' She pours herself some water from the glass jug on the table. 'You looked fucking *mental*.'

'Yeah – okay,' I say, frustration bubbling back up. 'So I was wasted and mental. What the fuck happened?'

'Well,' says Lucy and I can see she's starting to enjoy herself. 'Miguel starts asking me what's going on and... you know he's been to prison for assault and that don't you?' She pauses for effect. 'Well he starts asking what's going on and I ask you if you're okay again and you just blink and look at me and then back at him.

'Now Miguel starts getting a bit crazy too because he's wasted as well and, you know, he's a bit crazy anyway.'

'What the fuck was I doing? That just doesn't sound like me. He must have done something to piss me off.'

'He hardly even speaks English!'

'Yeah but it would have to take *something* to start me off like that!' My voice is getting louder, people are staring to look at us. 'He's like the hardest bastard in the place. Why would I want to fuck with him?'

Somewhere inside me there's a little spark of pride at not having picked an easy target though it's nothing compared to the blanket of confused shame smothering me.

The waiter turns up with our food and stands there wringing his hands. After a second he asks if we need anything else. I shake my head and force a smile and he retreats to the bar and watches us.

'What the fuck is he looking at?' asks Lucy.

'Now who's the fucking psycho?' I ask her through a mouthful of toast but she doesn't even smile. 'What happened then?'

'Well,' she goes on, 'Miguel starts staring back at you and you go on staring at him and then you just get up and walk away. I don't know where you went but while you're gone Miguel gets all paranoid and starts talking about getting a knife and stuff. Then you come back and your hand's all mashed and bleeding and Miguel disappears and comes back with a fucking kitchen knife.'

'Jesus,' I'm wallowing in a sea of cringe now. 'Did he go for me?'

'Well he fucking tried to,' says Lucy. The waiter is still watching us. 'I got in front of him and took the knife off him. Then Matty turned up from nowhere and started holding you back.'

'What was I saying?' I ask, mystified as to why I'd be behaving like that.

'You weren't really saying anything. You just had this fucking psycho look in your eyes and you were telling Matty to let you go, but you weren't saying it loud or anything. You were just going "Matty let go, Matty let go" in a quiet voice but your eyes were crazy and you wouldn't stop staring at Miguel.'

'Fuck.' I shudder and all of a sudden it's unbearable to listen to. I'm not that person. I don't do stuff like that. I'm in control.

I lost control.

'What happened then?' I say in a quieter voice and I can't look at her.

'Well I took the knife off Miguel and then I was hugging him round the waist and you were still talking to Matty and I felt another knife in the back of Miguel's belt and I took that away too. By now there were loads of people watching and Miguel was going fucking ape-shit and you were starting to calm down a bit so I pushed him into another room and came back to help Matty put you to bed.'

'It's lucky he let you take him away.' I cover my face with my hands, looking through my fingers at the yellow yolks hardening on my plate.

'It's lucky you chilled out a bit. You're a fucking psycho man. I've never seen you like that before. You scared the shit out of us.'

I stay there for a long time, rubbing my eyes with my finger tips, resting my chin on my palms. This is the last straw. I have to sort myself out. I have to stop this merry-go-round of

emotional suppression and self-abuse. I have to take
responsibility for myself.

But it hurts, Mum, it hurts and it's bad.

But I have to do it. Now. Or I'm fucked.

'I'm so sorry, Lou,' I say slowly, my eyes closed. Then
straighten up and spread my hands flat on the table. I look
up, look her in the eye and say it again:

'I'm so sorry.'

She meets my eyes and holds the look for a few seconds
trying to read me. Inside my guts a voice croaks out: *Why are
you looking for forgiveness from her? She's fucked up many
more times than you have. What right has she got to judge you*

I listen to the voice and then answer it with another
warmer one: *I need some kind of forgiveness. For Mandy, for
last night and for god knows how many other nights. I need to
stop being such a fuckhead and sort myself out before something
bad happens.*

The first voice is silent. The sounds of teacups clinking, of
cutlery on plates, of murmured conversation float back to me.
Lucy's eyes come back into focus. I smile.

'I'm sorry, Lou,' I say again and this time I'm wide open,
this time I'm sincere. She smiles.

'That's okay, Wil,' she says and takes my hand across the
table. 'Just don't do it again. You scared the shit out of me.'

That evening I'm cooking spaghetti for everyone in the
kitchen. The day has been a gruelling tour of humble pie and
apologies. I'm stuffed with the former and drained by the
latter.

I still feel my whole body cringing, but there's an
acceptance to it now. I feel purged. I feel like I've reached a
turning point and the first twitches of optimism are
germinating in me.

I was even nice to Mandy. I gave her a hug and asked her if she was okay. She looked better. She denied having talked to herself, but other people confirmed it. She needs to get out too.

I put my cigarette in the ashtray and grate parmesan into a bowl. I can hear people starting to get drunk out in reception, laughter and glasses clinking. I sip my cup of tea and for the first time I feel that there may be a little normality creeping back into me. I smile.

The door opens. It's Miguel. He stops and looks at me. I look at him, my teacup frozen in mid sip.

We stay like that for a moment. Not really sizing each other up, both of us just waiting for the other to react. I let my eyes drop and bow my head slightly. In my peripheral vision I see him relax; he exhales and his shoulders drop a millimetre.

'I'm sorry, Miguel,' I say in Spanish, my eyes still lowered. '*Lo siento.*'

He's quiet for a minute then he says, in English, 'I'm sorry too.'

We both know it's over now and immediately we're like a pair of schoolboys after a fight. The both of us stripped of our bravado, humbled.

I want to ask him what he remembers. I want to ask him if he really would have stabbed me. But my Spanish isn't good enough, nor is his English, and so we both smile shyly and blink lots.

Then he says, 'Excuse me,' and heads for the fridge and I say,

'No, excuse me,' and I back away and bustle about doing nothing. When he's half way out the door I call to him.

'*Gracias*,' I say.

'*De nada*,' he says and gives me a little wink.

29: 'On stubby wings the days then crouch
and on each day new plumes I try,
until my bald and pimpled soul
is fledgling ready now to fly.'

Earl Weathers

Buenos Aires rumbles on and life rumbles on with it. I was only planning to stay here a couple of weeks, but I've been here a month already. My capacity for self-abuse is dwindling, my patience for hangovers is almost exhausted and it's nearly time to pack up and move on, nearly...

One morning, when the sun shone wan and weak through the fuzz of city smog, Mandy and I sat on the roof and said our goodbyes for the last time. We hadn't spoken much during our time in the Orange Tree and when we did our conversations were generally steeped in guilt and resentment. It wasn't a happy goodbye, of course, but we'd drawn it out over so many weeks that any goodbye would have been welcome.

She forgave me. I forgave her. I asked her tactfully how she felt since the night she was talking to herself. Again she denied it. We nearly argued about it but instead we hugged a short and awkward hug, and then she left. She's in Brazil. I hope she's happier.

Life changed as soon as Mandy left. The gnawing guilt left my guts and in a sense I felt free. But it was still a hungover freedom, a coked-up freedom and a freedom moving too fast to really call my own.

After my night of craziness I forced some kind of normality on myself, I cooked lots and drank less. I snorted half as much and tried to watch what I said and how I acted.

For two days Lucy gave me a hard time and then we settled back into our old roles. She had a job, teaching English at a publishing house on the tenth floor of a tower block. She was waking up early and wearing smarter clothes and, though her weekends were no less flamboyant, she seemed much happier.

As soon as Lucy let me off the hook everyone else seemed to do the same. She tells the story of that night to newcomers, exaggerating and embellishing it a little more with every telling. By now it sounds like we had some kind of medieval duel, and for all I remember we might have done.

Miguel and I have forged some kind of uncommunicative friendship, after he nearly stabbed me, and I nearly asked him to; sometimes he invites me for a smoke on the roof or in his clothes-strewn room and we make polite, pidgin conversation and smile shyly at each other. As I said, he's a dangerous guy, but a good one none the less.

And so Buenos Aires rumbles on and I ramble on with it. Other than hedonism there seems to be little reason for my existence here, and hedonism was never much of a reason to exist anywhere for me.

But that brings me, in a roundabout sort of way, to Em Kennedy. If life is a series of junctions, and coincidences are its signposts, then the coincidence that got us talking is the size of a billboard. But I'll start from the beginning...

It's an odd time: those first few days of semi-normality and social paranoia when all I want to do is make everyone like me again. I want to impress on them that I'm not a weirdo or a psycho. I want them to know that I'm not dangerous or strange. I just want what everyone else wants: to be loved.

So I act as naturally as possible, which is to say I act rather unnaturally because I'm trying too hard to be natural. I keep biting off the ends off my sentences because the censors in my brain have deemed them too risqué, rude, violent or insensitive to finish. I'm smiling and helping out too much, and probably seem as weird, if not weirder than I was before.

Matty and Aaron have gone north to see the Iguazú falls so I'm hanging out with Tim and Mylo. They don't care that I lost it that night so I don't have to be too nice to them. In fact they're the only ones I'm actually being normal with.

Anyway, the three of us are playing pool in the afternoon. The sun is shining through the trees by the window. As ever the road outside is throbbing and roaring away. Apart from that the hostel is quiet. Out of respect for this rare outbreak of peace, we're being quiet too, only occasionally raising our voices for a good shot or a bad miss.

The doorbell buzzes and Maria tuts and sighs and tears herself away from her magazine to press the entry button. The door downstairs wheezes open and bangs shut again and footsteps come running up the stairs. Tim is bent down to plant the white into a red and that red into another red and that red into the middle left pocket. He's frowning with concentration and waiting for the person to hurry up and come in.

Mylo is standing by the window watching some policemen on the corner who are watching some raggedy kids hanging out on the grass verge. I'm sitting on the radiator, rolling a cigarette with a pool cue between my legs. I'm half watching the door to see who'll come in, and half watching Tim's over-ambitious pool shot – he's never going to make it.

The footsteps stop at the top of the stairs and the top doorbell goes and I can hear Maria complaining again. The door is just out of my line of sight around the corner but Tim can see it. The frown of concentration on his face melts as he watches the person walk in. I lean forward to see who it is and the pool cue slips forward with me and knocks the cigarette out of my hand. I bend down to pick it up, then I look towards the reception desk and the new arrival. It's Em, Em Kennedy.

And so begins this next chapter of this story, so darkness lightens up, so pain starts to become pleasure.

She's Irish, is Em. Five foot five and bouncing off the ceiling. She has a compact energy about her which fizzes and crackles and gives off little sparks. She's a graff artist and a primary school teacher, a former child gymnast and a peroxide blonde. She speaks Spanish like an Irish pikey and spends most of her life dancing on the spot. She's small, bouncy, bubbly and friends with everyone.

To be honest, the first time I saw her all I noticed was her pert little butt. But the energy was sensed, man, sensed by everyone.

Mylo isn't watching the coppers any more, Tim looks back at his pool shot, distractedly pulls back his cue arm and gently swings it forward again. He makes the plant perfectly. Out of the corner of my eye I see him do it, but he doesn't even look round for recognition. While Em chats to Maria the three of us are frozen, gawping statues. Then the spell snaps, Em turns around and walks over to us.

'Hello there lads,' in lovely, lilting brogue.

Caught a little off guard by the sudden reanimation of life, the three of us cough and shuffle and clear our throats.

'Hello,' says Tim. Suddenly remembering that he made the plant he points at the table and raises his eyebrows at me. I nod but it's not really in recognition.

'Alright,' I say to Em and I'm suddenly nervous and twitchy, but I'm smiling like a goon. Big Mylo says nothing, he just grins and turns rosy red and nods at her.

'D'you have a cigarette I could pinch?' she asks, smiling at the three of us, bouncing on the spot in a way which would make anyone else look a little crazy. Of course we have a cigarette, all three of us do. Em takes one from Mylo, who blushes even deeper, and I lean forward to light it for her.

'Tanks fellers,' she says, smiles at us all and turns on her heels. We stand dumbly where she left us and watch her go.

A few nights later a bunch of us are drinking by the fire in reception. Em and her friend Pablo are here. It's a pleasant evening, apart from the fact that Em has a friend. In fact I'm gutted that Em has a friend. Nevertheless, it's been a pleasant evening and I'm being as friendly and polite as I can.

Pablo seems a nice enough guy, we're drinking and sharing cigarettes and chatting. I'm talking to him because otherwise I'd be jealous and giving him bad vibes. I find it much easier to be friendly in these situations. Keep your friends close and your enemies closer, as the man says.

I'm grudgingly starting to like him, though there is an odd intensity to him. It's as if he's got angry-short-man syndrome, but he's not really that short. I can't quite work him out.

We share another beer and he mentions a friend of his who's a model, and I mention a guy from Buenos Aires who I shared an apartment with in Milan back in 2001. We were there to do shows, hundreds of us from all over the world, taking over Milan and Paris for a couple of weeks at a time, smoking weed in Louis Vuitton HQ and hanging out with rich, arrogant fashionistas. I can't remember the guy's name, but I describe him to Pablo; he's about six foot something, has dark hair and eyes, skates, writes graff, drinks yerba maté and smiles a lot.

There are fifteen million people in Buenos Aires. There must be hundreds of male models from here.

'His name is Dario,' Pablo's dark face lights up. 'He is my best friend.'

The mind is really boggling now. I search around in its memories for the guy's name. It is Dario. I'm sure it is.

'Does he carry a camera with him all the time?' I ask, I still can't believe it. 'Does he take sly pictures of tramps and junkies and stuff like that?'

'It is Dario! He's always doing that!'

'No shit? That's too crazy. Where is he? Is he in here? I love that guy.'

Suddenly my enemy has become my friend's friend. I'm sure there's a proverb in there somewhere.

'Em!' Pablo calls across the room. She comes bouncing over and stands in front of us, grinning expectantly. Her mouth is slightly too big for her face, but she makes that look good too – everyone else's mouths are too small. The pair of us grin up at her, boggled, gob-smacked.

'This guy knows Dario,' says Pablo. 'They were together in Milan. It's crazy!'

Much enthusiasm ensues, much amazed laugher and much disbelief. It turns out that Em is renting a corner of Dario's garage as a studio. Pablo lives with his mum and brothers in the flat upstairs, Dario lives downstairs with his girlfriend and their dog.

'The mind boggles,' we say and we shake our heads.

'What are the chances?' we ask and we sigh in awe.

'It's a small world,' we say and roll our eyes.

It's not a small world. I've seen some of it and it's huge. Massive. There are more than six billion people in it. 6,000,000,000 people! There's something else going on, something we don't know about. Something big. Sometimes things just happen. Maybe the things are always happening...

I look at Em and I smile.

Em looks at me and she smiles.

Pablo looks at both of us.

We're smiling at each other.

Pablo doesn't smile.

Pablo doesn't smile at all.

That night ended as many do, with me in my own bed and Em in another. In the morning I wake up thinking about her. I realise that I'm feeling unusually bouncy. Tentatively I lower myself off the bunk and try a little dance-on-the-spot. It feels good. I try smiling. That feels good too.

Last night's booze is hanging around my neck like a musty little mink. I shrug, the mink leaps in the air and then settles back down again. I try all three at once – smiling, shrugging and dancing on the spot – the mink leaps in the air again, but this time it disappears. I still feel a little fuzzy but it's more like a caterpillar's moustache tickling my temples than a frowsy, dead vermin.

Caterpillar's moustaches I can live with, they're alright.

I wander around the room in my pants, getting clothes and shower stuff together, I try a little hum, it feels nice. I try a little song:

'... but now I'm feeling so much better

I could cakewalk into town...'

That feels nice too.

A head pokes out from a grubby sleeping bag at eye level with my crotch,

'Shuddup!' says the head.

'Fuck you, my man,' I tell the head with a smile and a jiggle and I dance off to the bathroom

Showered, clean and clothed I run downstairs to order my morning coffee. The guy behind the counter watches me warily.

'Is there something wrong with you?' he asks in Spanish, his eyes narrowing.

'Why?' I ask, smiling at him, making eye contact. That in itself is unusual for this time of day.

'You seem... happy,' he says and he pronounces the word

like it tastes bad. 'You're not usually happy until much later.'

'I'm not happy,' says me, still smiling and bouncing a little.

'Oh,' he frowns and shakes his head. I leave him a peso tip and skip back upstairs.

I sit on the couch and drink my coffee, black, two sugars. Maria and I exchange a couple of good natured insults. She smells, I smell, etc.

The doorbell goes and a second later Em walks in. She isn't looking too bouncy. Maybe the mink landed on her.

'Good morning.' My heart nudges my ribcage like a bag of frogs.

'Good morning,' she says back and plops herself down next to me, making the couch jump and groan a little. She pinches one of my ciggies. I light it for her and lean back and stretch a good stretch, hooking my thumbs together like a diver. It's a bit of a theatrical stretch, to hide the fact that I don't really know what to say next. I try a yawn: the drama yawn. I almost complete the move by letting my arm fall onto the couch behind her head, but I abort due to unusually high levels of cheesiness.

'I want to talk to you about something you said last night,' she says after a while.

I cringe. Of course I cringe. What the fuck did I say? She doesn't look happy.

'Oh yeah?' I say, cool as a cucumber in a sauna. 'What's that then?'

'You said something about Pablo,' she says, her bonnie blue eyes all worried and downcast. 'You said you weren't sure about him. You worried me a bit.'

'Oh shit.' I'm glad I didn't do the cheesy arm thing, I'm cringing enough as it is. 'I'm sorry if I was out of order. I didn't mean any harm. He seems like a nice enough guy to me.'

'Oh, he's a nice guy,' she looks disappointed. 'It's just that I was getting some funny vibes off him too. I wondered what it was you saw?'

'Well...' I grope around in my brain 'he did seem quite territorial around you. Though I suppose that's okay.'

'That's the thing though, Wil,' she says, tapping her cigarette on the edge of the ashtray, 'we're not even together. He really wants us to be but we're not. We're just mates really.'

'Oh,' says me, nodding sympathetically, but inside I'm whooping and doing a lap of honour. I try not to let it show. It does.

'So you're not together but he's still being possessive?' I clear my throat and frown like I imagine a doctor or a shrink would. 'That's not cool. Are you staying with him?'

'Yeah,' she says, 'but we're not sleeping together. Just sharing a bed sometimes.'

'Hmmm,' I nod sagely, scheming all the while, 'I can see where he's coming from. If I fancied the pants off you and you were sleeping in my bed I think I might get a bit stressed out and jealous too.' She looks at me when I say that, a quick, searching look. 'How jealous does he get?' I ask.

'That's the thing,' says Em, frowning like a puppy, 'he can be quite weird about it sometimes. He's a bit scary when he's drunk.'

'Has he... done anything?'

'Oh no, no, no!' She says, shaking her head. 'No, nothing like that. He's just a bit of a weirdo.'

'Hmmm,' still nodding sagely. 'Do you have a bed here?'

'Yeah.' She crosses her legs and turns round in her seat to face me, giving me the whole body language thing. 'But I don't like hostels much, you know?'

'Yeah, I know,' says me, smiling and turning round towards her a little more, 'but maybe it's better than the alternative, just for a couple of days.'

'You're probably right,' she puts her hand on my knee. 'Thanks a lot, Wil, you're a star.'

'No worries,' says me, still smiling. 'How's Dario, by the way? I can't wait to see him.'

'He's great,' she says, grinning back. 'I can't believe you guys know each other, that's such a coincidence, isn't it?'

'It's all meant to happen,' says me with a wink.

But there's fear in me still, however cocksure I sound.

The Mandy scenario dented my ego because I didn't think I was the type to drag out a bad situation for so long. The Miguel debacle stole some of my self-confidence because I didn't think I was the type to lose control like that. The coke has robbed me of my endorphins and the weed has inhibited my mind and made me paranoid.

So the Em situation scares me a bit, I have to be honest. I'm scared because I don't want another Mandy-and-Wil on my hands. I'm scared because I don't want to suddenly manifest a heartful of feelings which I then have to bottle up and dispose of when I move on again.

I suppose I'm scared of rejection too. What if she's just being nice? What if she doesn't fancy me? What if I'm not good enough? What if she sees me for the weak, scheming bastard that I am?

What if? If not? Not if? If... what?

I don't think I can blame all these fears on recent events either. In fact, if I look deep into myself, it's obvious that I've been carrying them around since I first realised that I had a heart and a dick. The same nonsense fears surface every time I start liking a girl, and the ways I deal with them are wrong and many: Sometimes I give in to my fear and paranoia, quickly destroying the relationship by being too weak and needy, or I convince myself and my partner that I'm not worth the time or the effort. Sometimes I convince myself, wrongly or otherwise, that I don't really give a fuck so I end up being aloof and unresponsive, and ultimately kill myself with the guilt of being a bastard (see 'The Mandy Method').

Never have I relaxed and let go. Never have I let my emotional doors swing open and said '... to hell with the consequences'. Never have I been brave enough to put my nuts on the line and say 'Hey. This is me. This is it and that's all. This is how I feel. I am weak and I'm scared but I am fundamentally a good person, full of love and strength and all I need you to do is love me back and we'll be fine.'

Consequently never have I truly loved. Except for from a distance, from behind an emotional boulder or in weeping retrospect.

I am, truthfully, woefully, pathetically yours: Mr W. G. Coward.

It's a jungle out there, but I *want* to play Russian roulette with fluffy pink bullets. I want to gamble on this tacky, poison Wheel-of-Fortune love game. I want to let go, I really do. It almost seems rational. Better to have loved and lost. Better to have pulled the trigger and got a faceful of heart shaped shrapnel. Better to spin the wheel and bust out than... what? Perpetual singlehood? Eternal onanism? Give me love or give me death or give me dying trying...

But I'm scared. I'm shitting myself. So what do you do, Mr C? What do you do?

Here's what you do. You wait for a time when Em's on her own and you wander up to her and casually you say, like you don't give a fuck if she says yes or no, you say:

'I'm bored. What are you up to?' And she looks up and before she has a chance to answer you say, 'D'you wanna come for a drink with me?'

And you bite back the words that want to tumble out, words

that want to babble and froth: 'I don't mean anything funny or anything, just a drink, nothing else. I don't even like you that much, unless you like me, in which case I do like you...'

You bite those buggers back and you wait, biting your lip, flicking through expressions like a cinemascope and then, thank the fucking lord, she smiles and in husky brogue she says:

'Sure I'd love to come, just let me get my shit together.'

Then you sit yourself happily down on the couch and you light a cigarette so that you don't do a screaming Klinsman along the reception desk, and you breathe, and you take stock: You've faced your fear. You've made the first step. You feel exposed but the excitement and elation makes up for that. This is good. This is how it's done. Just stay loose, breathe and keep letting go...

Then you wander through the purple early evening streets and the brooding clouds seem light and airy and the snarling traffic seems to hum and purr. You wander up beside tall trees hissing softly in the wind and you find a bar where you can both imagine yourselves drinking. Then you sit opposite each other across a wooden table, and the waitress brings a basket of popcorn and two frothy beers, sweating in frozen glasses. You bite back your fears and you smile and they melt away.

She's easy to talk to and you talk and crunch popcorn and you watch people passing by. The people on the buses watch you and you make eye contact with them for a stalled second without communication, and then they're gone.

She tells you what she does and what she wants to do and you tell her the same things about yourself. You tell her the truth and it feels like facing your fear and you're not play-acting. She listens and she gets it and you get it and it makes you both happy.

The beers make you happy too and so you have some more

and when she goes to the toilet you watch her go. You don't make eyes at the waitress. You just watch the world go by and marvel at the solid harmony between your guts, your brain and your dick.

When she comes back you're looking serious and she asks you what's wrong and you resist the temptation to tell her about the loneliness in you. Instead you smile and she smiles and you get another beer and it all keeps flowing just right.

Then you need another bar because this one and its basket of un-popped popcorn is getting bored of you. So you jump into a cab, giggling. You're only wearing shorts and T-shirt because you thought you were only coming out for one or two, but it doesn't matter. She says she'll keep you warm and that makes your heart and dick twitch and you smile secret smiles that the cabbie doesn't know about and that's as cosy as it gets.

In the old part of the city you find a bar you found once when you were alone. A bar old and high-ceilinged and blackened-oak, which flows milky white light onto a little cobbled square. It looks like the whole scene has been lifted from times long dead, when life was good and smelled of leather, pomade and carbolic soap.

You're quieter here and more intimate. The basket is full of monkey nuts now and you sit closer together and watch through the high windows the crazy man in full jungle cammo whose self-appointed job it is to look after people's parked cars. You take it in turns to dub his conversations with the intimidated people who park in his zone and you laugh private laughs like the other antique couples in the room. The beer just won't stop flowing good and fear is faced and passed and that heart shaped chamber in the fluffy gun was empty, and all the hammer did was click like there was nothing to be scared of all along. And then, when the past and the monkey nuts have had their fill of you, you move on. This time you hold hands in the street and laugh and almost kiss and then laugh again and run like kids in a hay field. Even the cops on the corners are happy. Even the pickpockets and hookers are clean and shiny.

It's getting late or early now but the sky is still dark. You bustle almost by mistake into another place because the bouncer liked your faces and it's so grand and huge the two of you are almost dwarfed by it. You stop and gawp and hold each other, taking in the white marble staircases and five floors of bars and chandeliers and old world opulence.

She's wearing a hoodie and you're wearing shorts and a T-shirt but nobody suit-and-tie cares. She gets drinks while you take a piss and in the toilet a man with an afro and a girl dressed like a flapper are shouting politics at each other. It's almost too kitsch and too blatant in its naked clichés, so you come back a little confused and Em's confused too. The pair of you perch on one massive armchair and watch it all, a little bowled over but safe with each other. You drink your caipirinhas, picking mint out of each other's teeth, and then you leave quickly because it's all too much.

You walk slower and you hold hands, but you don't swing your arms any more and the ragged clouds are turning slowly blood red in between the buildings and the stars are still twinkling at the other end of the sky.

Then you wander into a bar you know will be dark and safe for one more nightcap because neither of you has fully let go yet, and it'd be odd to go home before you did.

So you sit quietly and sip your last drinks and you try to work up some kind of completion and the only way is either kiss her or tell her you're too scared to. You've been here so many times before and you talk into her ear and suddenly you start to fuck it all up. You tell her that maybe you and her aren't a good idea because you're going away next week, and your eyes are dying from what you're saying, but somehow you believe it because it means you don't have to get hurt.

She's nodding and her eyes are sad too. You hate yourself for being such a coward and you gulp your beer because you don't know what else to do. You know that it's all fucked again, the way it always was and it's you that fucked it.

The desperate gulf between yourself and yourself creaks open again, that vicious gap between sense and what you want flaps black and gaping and you know it's always going to be like this. You know you can't face your fear and not shrink and lose it in the end, and for a few seconds you are a desperate man, a pathetic, woeful man.

Then she leans towards you and lays her head on your shoulder and whispers in your ear:

'You're probably right. We probably would end up getting hurt. But it's such a shame, Wil. I've been wondering all night what it'd be like to kiss you.'

And your cowardice tears at you. You feel so stupid and naïve... You smell her hair and it smells so good, so good you take a deep breath and all of a sudden you're letting go, and you smile and all the fear falls away and vanishes, leaving nothing but you and her and the dim sounds of the bar. You turn your head and hold her soft, warm cheek and you kiss her. You kiss her and everything is okay. Because she does like you and you are okay. Maybe you'll get hurt. Maybe you'll get hit by a bus. It doesn't matter. It doesn't matter because everything's going to be alright now, everything's going to be just fine.

Then you walk slowly home, past the sleeping bums and the early birds and the light in the west spreading pink and purple in the cold breeze. Now and then you stop for a kiss and the kisses are slow and they mean so much and you both giggle a little at your fear and the fact you nearly messed it all up. But that's gone now and you wander on again.

Wander on and home and undress slowly and in a bunk for one, with the early morning sun peeping through the blinds, she lies down soft and white and naked, and you lie beside her and hold her and everything's going to be alright...

30: 'Now we rise and we are everywhere.' Nick Drake

To open my eyes again is no great thing, all it takes is the smallest, fastest reflex my body possesses. The flick of a tiny switch, a backwards blink, that is all. But to open my eyes this morning will be glorious, slow and tender, and I already know how delicious it will be.

I float slowly, sensuously towards awakening. First the nerves in my body realise where I am, who I'm with. There is a thigh resting on mine, a soft, warm thigh. There is an arm across my chest, a breast, a nipple, a palm small and light, fingers gentle. Resting on my shoulder there is a head, hair spilled, tumbled, tickling my arm. My eyes are closed but I can see her, my nerves whisper her to me. They tell me that she's breathing slowly and deeply, that she's peaceful, that she's happy where she is, that this won't be an awkward awakening, that when she wakes up she will smile.

I slide my left hand up to her sheet-covered hip and she wriggles closer to me. With my right hand I stroke her hair and she sighs and I feel her smile against the skin of my shoulder.

Then I open my eyes, slowly, happily, one at a time, savouring each tangled eyelash, each soft-focus eye-water bent bubble of light, until it clears, until I see her lying there, small and light and beautiful, entwined in crumpled sheets and blonde hair... I smile... inside me something moves, something hot and wholesome and comfortable, yet something huge. It rises up in my guts like a golden ball of hummingbirds and it settles there, glowing and vibrating, sending sweet shocks of light through my nerves, glowing on the walls and on the bed, glowing on the ceiling and out the window, filling the room and the world and me... and I smile. I smile without thinking about smiling, I smile because I'm happy.

... And then she wakes up and she kisses me, and then there is no world illuminated, but an illumination which just happens to contain a world... and us...

It takes a lot of effort and a lot of hunger to eventually push us out of bed and back into the world. It's almost dark by the time we rise. We limp to the bathroom for showers, both of us grinning dull happiness, all edges smoothed, all colours mellowed, all tension removed and removed again.

On the couches by the fire the drinking has started and the music and laughter is loud. We drift in like happy ghosts to haunt our friends. We watch each other and smile. We laugh with the others, and at first they try laughing at us, but seeing that no rise can be got out of either of us, happily they give up. Soon the glow affects them too, soon that beautiful hum spills out into the room, crowds out all awkwardness and stress, leaving us all warm and glowing though most of them don't even know why.

The following week is almost all bathed in that glow. In my mind it's another happy montage scene of pastel colours and perfect smiles. The sun never stops shining even though it rains an awful lot.

It even shines the night of the big storm, when Matty and Aaron return. A bunch of us are smoking joints on the rainy roof, watching the sheet lightning and the fork lightning and every kind of lightning I can imagine, all brought together for one fantastic display, cracking the charged air and sending sudden towers of steam like twisters drifting across the black and brooding sky, the skyline alive for a second; a tower here, a church steeple there, thumped viciously by a branch of magnesium-bright light.

All of us stand in a dripping line, our mouths hanging open in awe, passing soggy joints. Em, beautiful with her hair falling wet across her face.

Then a crack and a searing flash comes almost simultaneously, smacking a building across the street like an electric rattlesnake. We cheer and howl and run around like dogs do in a thunder storm. A second later all the power for our block and the blocks around us goes down – buildings, streetlights, traffic lights all plunged suddenly into darkness, lit up sporadically and violently, casting random shadows, dancing in conflicting directions.

As one we realise what's happened and what it means; just below us is the biggest road in the world, eighteen lanes of traffic, hundreds of traffic lights and junctions, all delicately managed by some intricate computer system, all useless now. We crowd together against the low roof wall, looking down onto the road. Below us the traffic hisses by in water standing an inch deep. Nothing has happened yet, the road behaves as it ought to, as if it still remembers what order is. Then a car on a crossroad comes flying though, brakes squeal, lights spin and cars pirouette delicately, almost lazily across the road. Then other cars fly by, each missing the other by the smallest chance, every single one missing the others by some amazing fluke. There isn't much noise, no crashing, not many horns, just the squeal of breaks and the sucking hiss of tyres.

We watch, completely lost in it, barely speaking, covering our mouths and,

'Oh shit, this one has to...'

Covering our eyes, peaking out from between our fingers,

'Oh my god how did he miss… ?'

For ten minutes we watch those tons of metal-encased flesh career by, cars dancing like matadors, trucks like elephant ballet, headlights circling like searchlights, the sky flashing and charged, the air sodden and crackling.

And then the light comes back – blink, blink, back on. The world swings back from the edge. The darkness and the insanity just blink away. The cars stop dancing and the streetlights catch the pavements with their orange pools and long shadows just before it seemed that they would slip away entirely.

Then the clouds lumber out towards the coast and the lightning walks with them, out and away, marching and grumbling into the distance. The rain stops and we looked at each other, laughing, rosy-cheeked and exhilarated.

But it isn't the near danger that impressed us. It's the near chaos, that darkness and light, that sudden absence of colour and abundance of energy and then the sudden re-emergence of order. As if chaos is always there, masked thinly by the illusion of order. As if nature was just letting us know: 'I don't have to let you do this to me, you know. I don't have to tolerate you.'

And all we can do is stand there and gawp until she's finished, useless and small and gaping in awe, dripping and impressed and entirely humbled.

I could go on like this. I could settle here for a while, with Em and Buenos Aires, now that self-abuse has become what it should be: a thing to take lightly and to indulge in only rarely and only in moderation, so that it is fun rather than punishment.

I could get myself an apartment somewhere in La Boca, I could hang out with Dario and the BA crowd, skaters and artists, musicians and models. I could set myself up and forge a life for myself. I'm thinking seriously about it.

But something holds me back, something simple and heavy, a weight and a knowledge: I am tired. I am tired of living out of a backpack, I'm tired of not having a home, I'm tired of not having old friends and family, I'm tired of being a stranger. I'm tired like I was of high altitude, like I was of dust.

I've experienced so much over the past six months and had so little time to digest it. I feel full of it, weighed down by it. I need to stop for a while. I need some space to think and remember who I was and to know who I am now.

Em understands. We're sitting on hard-backed bus seats on the way back from seeing her studio and Dario in La Boca, still basking in the warm glow of seeing an old buddy and getting a feel of what real life is like in this crazy city; stencils and home-made skate ramps in garages and drug dealers on the corners and real people's homes after so many weeks in hostels and tents.

'When do you fly out?' she asks, playing with my finger, pulling at the little hairs between the knuckle and the first joint.

'I've got to be in Santiago in a couple of weeks.' I look down at her fingers, tiny and white compared to my big brown mitts.

'Chile,' she says.

'Uh-huh.'

Then she doesn't say anything for a while, just strokes my hand.

'I'm probably going to head over to Mendoza next week,' I say. 'Last time I was there the border kept getting closed because of snow in the Andes. It'll be worse now. I'd be smart to get there early.'

She just nods. Then she sighs and straightens herself up and she turns to me and smiles.

'Why don't I come to Mendoza with you?'

'That'd be fucking great,' I smile back at her. 'Have you been there before?'

'Nope,' she says, lifting my hand to her mouth and biting my finger, watching with cheeky eyes to see how much it'll hurt.

And so it's time, time to start saying goodbye. We leave Buenos Aires tonight. Sixteen hours on a night bus across the plains to Mendoza. The first bus journey I'll have made in more than a month. I wonder whether I'll still be able to have a good night's sleep sitting up. I wonder if I'm doing the right thing...

The first proper goodbye is at breakfast. Matty and Aaron have insisted on paying. I'm on the tail end of a night out with Em and Dario. I suppose that was a goodbye too, but maybe it doesn't count because we'd barely had time to get to know each other again.

Aussie, Yank and Welshman, together again we sit at a long table and order pancakes and coffee and talk about travelling down through Argentina together. The conversation consists mostly of laughing at me and my occasional lapses of sanity and good taste. It's all funny in retrospect, my wobbly road to now.

They're good lads, these two. I'm convinced that Aaron will be president of the USA one day. Matty, I'm equally convinced, will always be Matty.

I hate saying goodbye, it's probably my least favourite form of human interaction. I never know what to do with myself. I have no idea what to do with my hands when people tell me how great it's been to meet me. I don't know where to look when they tell me we should definitely do it all again some time. I have absolutely no idea what to say when they tell me I should look them up if I'm ever in their neck of the woods.

It's not as if anything they've said isn't true, or that I think they're stupid for saying it. It's just that I find it all so needless and awkward. Of course I'll keep in touch, of course I'll visit them if I'm ever close, of course I won't forget them – they're my friends. It's what friends do. You don't need to say it!

In the end I just keep grinning and say pretty much the same things back to them. Then we stand about for another few seconds, prolonging the awkwardness, unable to walk away or say anything meaningful or even make eye contact without blushing. Then someone says:

'Right!'

And we all just run away from each other, embarrassed and confused.

Back at the hostel I sneak into my room and start the long job of packing and sorting myself out for the road. I'm out of practice. For a while I could pack my entire life neatly into my bag without an inch of wasted space in fifteen minutes. Now I can't believe it'll all go in.

Mylo and Tim, the Canadians, have already left, they're in Mendoza trying to make the pass over the mountains. They've reserved a room for me and Em in their hostel for tomorrow night. A nice, private double room with a bag of weed waiting for us. From now on we travel in style. Em is back at Pablo's, packing and saying goodbye.

Lucy looks in at the door and asks me how it's going. There's a hint of reproach in her voice, as if she's pissed off with me for leaving her again. I stand up and walk over to her. We look down at my gear arranged on the floor: fishing rod, Shining Path balaclavas from Peru, 'Chavez no se va!' T-shirt from Venezuela, cooking pots and worn out old clothes, stacks of pictures and scribbled notes. It's a sorry sight in a way, a weary sight. If I was at home looking at these things they'd seem unusual and exotic but now they just look tired and lonely.

'So what's your plan?' I ask her, putting my arm around her shoulder.

'I'm gonna stay here for a bit, I've got to make some cash,' she says. 'Though I don't know how good it'll be now you're all abandoning me.'

I stick my bottom lip out and she laughs.

'Och, I know,' she says, 'I'll be fine.'

'That's the spirit,' I say. 'I'll be going to my sister's in New Zealand for a while, just to rest up and play Uncle Wil. You're more than welcome there when you come through.'

'I'll keep in touch,' she says and we hug a big strong one, one of those ones that is accompanied by a big 'Aaargh' from both of us.

Then follow a million goodbyes, some good and casual, some awkward and embarrassing. Miguel and I square up in pantomime masculinity and make fake stabbing motions at each other. Then the shyness hits us both again. We shake hands formally and then hug properly. I like him but he is a bit of a crazy bastard...

And after all that, with our packs on our backs, we leave. Out of the light and the sentimental noises of the Orange Tree and into the gathering gloom of the city. We flag a cab outside and off we go. I look over at Em, she looks at me, and we hold hands all the way to the bus terminal, watching Buenos Aires streak by outside our windows, saying goodbye to all that too.

31: 'Nearly There. Nearly Where?' Heather Gumption

Wake up you two. Here's Mendoza again, almost leaf-bare and shivering now because it's cold, cold, cold.

Wake up Em, curled up blanket-snuffling against my pins-and-needles shoulder.

Then there's happy Mylo and Tim, welcome and more coffee.

And there's something else... something weird... hard to put my finger on it...

something

unusual...

it's...

it's...

silence...

Listen ... nothing....

No howling cars, no whining treble motorbikes, no dull rumble window-rattling heavy engine bass waves, no squealing breaks, no screeching fan belts, no horns, no sirens, no... nothing. It's blissful. Nothing is blissful.

Nothing is paradise.

Silence...

My heart slows down, my breathing deepens. I have time. I have space. I am relaxing. I am melting. My back straightens, my eyes brighten, my mouth turns up slightly at the edges and stays that way, my forehead becomes smooth, I am... chilling. I'm chilling!

I look over at the lads... they're chilling too... in fact they've got a head start on us, they're *really* chilling.

'Shall we... smoke a joint?'

'Has anyone got any papers?'

It's okay, they have papers, they have weed, they have wine, there's a supermarket just around the corner that sells the biggest, tastiest steaks we've ever eaten. It's okay, the hostel has a kitchen, a ping pong table, a little swimming pool full of ice and leaves, a big stone barbeque and a nice, big double room for me and Em.

Eventually the joint gets rolled and our things get unpacked and we retire to the chilly garden to smoke and play ping pong. The sun is shining and the air is crisp and brittle. The birds are singing and there is a mellow, ringing clarity to the world, like a crystal bong in a mountain waterfall. Like the Snow Queen's lacy undies. Like a slow-motion fire fight in a chandelier factory:

Mellowwwwwwwwwww.

Ping, pong, ping, pong all day long. Snuggle with Em, pong, ping, pong, little walk in the park, jays and stray dogs, pong, trees and silence, ping, peace, pong, supermarket, ping, steaks and potatoes, pong, good good red wine. On and ping pong on like a happy blurred dream world where everyone smiles and nobody cares who wins.

The border crossing is snowed over. Of course it's snowed over; it's up there at 3,500 metres above the sea in a little cleft between two towering, jagged, frozen mountains. There are glaciers up there, icicles as thick as a man, mammoths, sabretooth tigers, of course it's bloody closed!

'It may be open tomorrow,' says the unconvincing woman from the bus station in a lazy nasal drawl.

'Maybe?'

'Yes *Señor*, maybe,'

'I'll call back tomorrow then.'

'Yes *Señor*.' I hang up.

'It's still closed,' I tell everyone; they give a token sigh.

'Maybe tomorrow,' I say. It's been the same every morning for four days.

'Can't be helped,' says someone.

'Nothing we can do.'

'Skin up.'

'Wil,' says Em, 'shall we do something today?'

'Sure honey pie,' I say as enthusiastically as I can. I'm just so mellowwww. 'What kind of thing were you thinking of?'

'Dunno,' says Em. She's getting bored.

'Right!' says me, action stations. 'Skiing?'

She shakes her head quickly, doing that bouncing on the spot thing.

'Zoo?' I ask Em. She makes a face, a poor-animals-in-cages face.

'It'll be fun,' I say, giving it the two-thumbs-up and a grin. The animals-in-cages face turns into a kind-of-why-not face, which is followed by a vaguely enthusiastic nod.

'Zooooooo.'

On and on, the days go on like this, just happily plodding along. Each morning the woman from the bus station tells us to keep relaxing and each day we follow her orders to the syllable.

One morning is different though. Em has to go back to Buenos Aires. I knew it was coming, but I didn't want to think about it. Now it's crept up on me like a spiteful little boy with freckles and burst my bubble. Pop!

I'm pretending it's okay. I'm pretending to be strong and aware of fate and natural cycles of life and death and the rest of it, but I'm lying. I'm very sad.

Em and I are in bed. We're prolonging the morning-bed scenario because it seems that the best place to pretend to be strong is in bed in the morning. Neither of us is convinced.

We're being very lovely and friendly to each other and then we're quiet and a bit grumpy and then we have sex. Then we start all over again. We've been in bed all morning.

I don't like saying goodbye.

But Em's a good one, she's one of the best ones I've ever met. She knows how I feel about goodbyes and I haven't even told her about it. She just knows.

Before it's time for her to go she tells me how it's going to be:

'You don't have to come with me to the bus station,' she tells me, 'You can just come out and see me to a cab and pretend we'll be seeing each other again in a couple of hours. That way we don't have to get all weepy and silly.'

I feel so proud of her for saying that, I grab her and pick her up and give her a big squeeze and a kiss, then I feel all weepy and silly so I put her down again. She is lovely.

When the time comes our plan works perfectly and I don't feel silly at all until her taxi turns the corner and goes out of sight. Then I feel like I've lost an arm. I feel like I grew a new limb when we were together and now it's been torn off. It hurts quite a lot. I'm bleeding emotionally.

I walk back into the hostel and my emotional blood drips onto the floor and makes little puddles of sadness. Luckily no one has to clean it up, because it's not really there. Mylo and Tim can see that I'm wounded, so we open a bottle of wine and smoke our last spliff as if it was a special occasion: Emotional Amputee Day.

We're just about to begin the celebrations when the phone rings inside. The receptionist yells out to us:

'Wil! *Teléfono!*'

I excuse myself and dash indoors.

'Hello,' I say to the phone.

'Hello you,' says Em, 'I forgot to pay for my half of the room.'

In the bus station Em is standing beside her bus. Her bus is ready to go. Mylo and I are out of breath because our taxi drove so fast to get here. Mylo waves to Em and then pretends to look at magazines at a news-stand. I run over to her and pick her up again. It's like picking up my amputated limb and trying to put it back on for a few extra seconds. It doesn't really work, but it feels good anyway. Em and I are covered in blood and both of us have tears in our eyes. The bus driver beeps his horn at us. We kiss one last time. Then she pushes the money into my hand

and runs away. I watch her find a seat next to a fat man in a yellow shirt. I wave once and then I walk away, leaving the ghost of my lost limb twitching and thrashing around in the greasy diesel gunk and cigarette butts of the bus station floor.

Mylo and I don't really want to go home. We wander the streets for a bit. I feel lonely and a bit angry and I miss Em painfully. Mylo punches me on the arm. It hurts so I punch him back and then I smile. He smiles too.

'Chin up,' he says. We start walking faster then.

The bar is full of people associated with rugby. Oddly the under-twenty-ones' rugby world cup is being held here. They're in Mendoza from all over the world. They think we're crazy and adventurous for being here without guides and schedules. They think it's like the Amazon, or the moon or Bolivia, and they want to buy us drinks for being famous explorers. We tell them that we're just normal, but they buy us drinks anyway.

There are also some lads from Wales in the bar but they're a bit annoying. They have synthetic clothes fashionable only in small towns, and attitudes to match. I'd forgotten that people like that actually exist. They're convinced we're not famous explorers, and they don't seem to trust us, but that's okay because Mylo and I are too drunk to care.

'I really liked Em,' I tell Mylo much later. We're really drunk by now. I put my arm around his shoulder to keep myself from falling off my stool. It's getting very late. When we get home Tim is waiting up for us.

'Where have you been?' he asks. 'I was worried.'

He looks sleepy. He's in his pyjamas. Mylo and I are having trouble standing up.

'Em's gone home,' Mylo explains to Tim.

'And I was bleeding,' I explain, 'but I managed to staunch the wound.'

32: 'There are worse places to be than alone.' Ernest Hemingway

'Good morning', I say to the woman from the bus station.

'*Buenos dias, Señor,*' she says. This is how it always starts. We both know our lines off by heart.

'Are there any buses going to Santiago today?' I ask.

'*Si,*' she says.

'Oh,' I say. I wasn't ready for that. 'Er... em... What time is the next one?'

'Twelve and a half,' she says. She knows this part better than I do.

'Er... can I book a ticket for that one?'

'*Si,*' says the woman. 'You will be here half an hour early. Do not be late. Thank you.' The phone goes dead.

I look at the others. I forgot to get tickets for them. I scratch my head, then I say:

'The border's open.'

'Yes,' they say.

'I'm leaving at twelve thirty,' I say.

'Okay,' they say.

'I'd better pack,' I say.

'Yes.'

Tim looks at Mylo. Mylo looks at Tim.

'Shall we wait till tomorrow?' Tim asks Mylo.

'Okay.' Both of them look relieved. I look jealous.

'My flight...' I say.

'Yes,' they say.

I have a problem with saying goodbye. Now that I'm leaving, everything wants to say it to me and I have to say it to everything: Goodbye Mylo and Tim. Goodbye dirty-cream bitch (good girl, down girl). Goodbye hostel. Goodbye trees.

Goodbye streets. Goodbye statues. Goodbye tramps. Goodbye this. Goodbye that. Goodbye everything.

Hello bus.

As soon as I'm on it I feel better. It's not a very nice bus though. It reminds me of Peruvian buses. It smells of sour milk.

I'm alone now. My life is packed into two small bags and that's all I have. Just me and a few dusty, worn out things.

Chin up. I say to myself. Relax, let go, take it easy.

I relax. I let go. The engine starts. I fish out my headphones and MF Doom. Then I lie back, take it easy and watch Mendoza slide away outside my window.

Goodbye Mendoza.

On the long, dusty plain heading for the mountains the line of trucks begins. I don't know what it is at first, it's hard to fix perspective with the mountains so big and the road so straight. At first I think they're just rocks or boxes, hundreds and hundreds of them, all lining the side of the road. When we get closer I realise that they're trucks. Then the bus breaks down.

We sit by the side of the road and wait for another bus to come from Mendoza.

I feel brave and sad and lonely up here. I almost feel like a famous explorer, but then I hear some Irish lawyers talking in the seats behind me and I feel more normal again.

The road goes on and on. By now the snow is three metres deep and I can only see out of the window when we cross a bridge or a windy bit. The trucks are almost all covered in snow and the drivers look miserable. Sometimes we pass groups of them warming their hands by the big army ovens. The ground around them is littered with empty beer cans and rum bottles. Some of them have written their names in the snow. Maybe it's so someone will remember them if they never get out, Cristo, Fernando, Tajo all frozen and brittle.

Up at the border crossing most of the snow has been cleared by bulldozers. The crossing itself and the customs offices are underground, but it's still cold, cold enough to freeze a monkey's bum.

When the bus stops we all file off with our passports ready and our little forms filled out neatly with all the Xs in the right places. I always get nervous at border crossings. I'd be a terrible smuggler. I try to act normal, but I know that they can sense my fear, even though I've got nothing to be scared of – all my Xs are in the right places.

I join the queue behind the Irish people. They're not nervous at all. In fact they seem excited. It's like Butlins for them.

'No. I have nothing to declare,' I tell the bored woman behind the glass shield. She has a limp cigarette hanging out of her painted mouth. She doesn't believe a word I'm saying. 'No. I have no fruit or vegetables. No. I am not here to do terrorism. No. I am not a Nazi. Yes. I will only be in your country for two days. Thank you too.'

Then we all line up and watch while a man in rubber gloves and a man with a dog look through our luggage. My bag is like one of those Chinese paper pills which you put into water and a bear or a dragon pops out. If you open it it's hard to close again. The man with the rubber gloves is having trouble. I don't offer to help. I've made that mistake before and learned my lesson. I stand on my side of the yellow line and wince.

When we get back on the bus we're in Chile. Hello Chile.

I look at the new stamp in my passport. The woman behind the glass was as sloppy as she looked, the stamp is blurred and smudged. I'm so busy complaining to myself about her and the rubber glove man that I've forgotten to say goodbye to Argentina. I turn around in my seat and look out the window. The underground border looks cold and nasty like Hollywood Russia.

Goodbye Argentina. I think and I resist the Eva Peron temptation rising up in me.

When I look forward again there's a Chilean army officer coming up the bus towards me. He stops in front of me and asks me something. I'm so flustered that I don't understand him for a second, then I realise he's asking if he can sit next to me. I tell him it's fine and I try not to show how relieved I am that he doesn't want anything more serious of me.

'Are you okay?' he asks me when he's settled in.

'Yes,' I tell him. 'Tired and cold.'

'Oh yes,' he says and he says it in a way which makes me realise how tired and cold he must be.

'Cold and tired,' he says, like he's saying goodnight, and he puts his cap over his eyes and crosses his arms across his chest. After only five minutes of Chile he's snoring. After ten minutes of Chile I'm asleep too.

Santiago. It's dark, the bus station is full of hustlers, mangy dogs and armed police.

I smile and wave at the Irish lawyers, they wave back but they don't smile, they don't look very happy. Maybe they're waiting for the Redcoats to come and help them. I just smile and wave and head off into the crowd to find a taxi.

The hostel I've chosen to stay in, La Casa Roja, is a huge old colonial building in the middle of a street of other old colonial buildings. At the reception desk is a young gringo. I smile a grim hello and dump my pack on the floor with a grunt. I can hear people laughing and shouting in another room but it's quiet in here.

'*Hola joven*', I say to the gringo, who can't be more than eighteen.

'G'day,' he says to me.

'Got any rooms?' I ask, stretching and groaning.

'Maybe,' he says, looking at the computer. 'We're pretty full.'

'Anything,' I say and I look around the place. Same old, same old: rules and prices on handmade posters, daytrips and city tours, photos of happy, clean people having happy, clean fun. I'm starting to feel too old for this. Now that I'm going I want to just be gone.

'Got one in a ten bed dorm. Nothing else,' says the kid.

'I'll take it,'

I trudge upstairs and find the room. The lights are on. I push the door open and drag my pack inside. On the floor are seven or eight teenagers in sleeping bags, playing cards. Just looking at their fresh little faces makes me feel haggard and worn out.

'Hey guys,' I say, 'where's the spare bunk?'

'Hello,' they chorus. They all look a bit scared, one of the girls pulls her sleeping bag a bit further up to hide her pale little cleavage.

'What spare bunk?' One of the boys asks.

'This room nine?' I ask.

'Yes,' they chirp.

'Guy downstairs said there's a bunk for me.'

'Oh,' they gasp. I'm losing patience. I need a beer, a spliff and some time to chill. I don't need this.

'I'm going to leave my bag here,' I say and I walk down to reception. When I return with the reception kid they're sitting just how I left them, gawping.

'Who's in bunk seven?' asks the reception kid with practised annoyance. I notice he has a Kiwi accent.

'Sarah's got it,' says one of the girls in horsey English. The Kiwi looks at his clipboard.

'Sarah who?' he asks. I feel like banging my head against the wall.

'Sarah Forsyth,' says Horsey.

'She checked out today,' says the kid, then he turns to me. 'Bunk number seven,' he pats the unmade bunk and leaves.

'Thanks.' I dump my pack on the bunk and sit down heavily next to it. The kids on the floor try to imagine that I might not be there. They seem nervous. I want to ask them what's wrong. I want to tell them that it's okay, that there's nothing to be scared of. Poor kids, they must have only just arrived. Even the petrol station across the street must be scary for them. At the same time I'm enjoying their reaction. It makes me feel like a famous explorer.

I sigh and I lie back and rub my eyes for a bit. Then I put on my flip flops, say a polite but gruff goodnight to the kids and wander downstairs.

Half an hour later I'm feeling a bit better. I've had a beer and a moment to chill out, but I'm still feeling pretty ragged. My phantom Em limb is still there, wilted and heavy. I sit on a bench in the garden with the light and the noise of the kitchen shining on the privet bushes and roll a joint. Suddenly I feel small and tired and very, very lonely.

C'mon. I say to myself. *This time tomorrow we'll be out of South America and on the way to sister Josie's. A week in Tahiti first and then good old NZ for a proper rest. Nearly there, Willy.* Just one last push.

But I'm tired and I miss Em, I whinge.

But you're alive and strong and you've almost made it, I reply. Then I close my eyes and take a deep breath.

I love you, Wil, I say and that makes me feel much better. Then I open my eyes and light my joint and listen to the Aussie braying his story out to the whole world.

Just one more sleep…

The lights are out and the kids are snoring softly in room number nine. I pad barefoot to the bathroom, brush my teeth and then slip quietly into my sleeping bag.

I lie with my hands behind my head and think about my first night in South America. I think about that scared little boy, properly alone for the first time in years, listening to the ceiling fan and imagining the horror waiting for him outside in Caracas. I want to go back in time and tell him it'll be alright. I want to go back and give him a hug, but I know he doesn't need it; he did alright, didn't he?

I try to piece together my memories in chronological order, but I don't get very far. I'm only in Araguita with the family by the time I drift off to sleep, walking through that haphazard jungle with a shotgun and a bottle of Brujita, the butterflies like dinner plates and the bees humming in the flowers.

'The captain's turned on the seatbelt light. Please fasten you safety belts, put your seat backs in their original, upright positions and stow your tray tables for take off...'

Chile waddles by, picks up speed, flicks by, hurtles by and then disappears beneath us with a pleasant lurch.

I feel the last few sinews of the Em limb being torn away, the twinge as the little Mylo and Tim limb comes off, the Lucy limb, the Clara limb. It's just me now. Me, the world, and these phantom limbs drifting away to join other phantom limbs from the past. I'm like a sea anemone, waving my sad ghost tentacles at everything I've ever left behind.

Then I let go and I relax into my seat.

Then the excitement kicks in again.

I made it. That's all I can think. *I made it.*